Lektürehilfen

Nick Hornby

About a Boy

von Philip N. Hewitt

Klett Lerntraining

Philip N. Hewitt, M. A., langjähriger Englischlehrer in Großbritannien und Deutschland; freiberuflicher Übersetzer und Kurzgeschichtenautor.

Nick Hornbys Roman *About a Boy* (London: Penguin und Klett, 2000) liegt unter ISBN 978-3-12-573830-0 mit einem 18-seitigen Vokabelanhang als Klettbuch vor. Auf diese Ausgabe beziehen sich die Seitenangaben der Lektürehilfe.

9 783129 230039

Bibliografische Information der Deutschen Bibliothek
Die Deutsche Bibliothek verzeichnet diese Publikation in der Deutschen Nationalbibliografie; detaillierte bibliografische Daten sind im Internet über http://dnb.ddb.de abrufbar

Auflage 8. 7. 6. 5. | 2016 2015 2014 2013
Die letzten Zahlen bezeichnen jeweils die Auflage und das Jahr des Druckes.

1. Auflage 2005
Internetadresse: http://www.klett.de/lernhilfen
Umschlagfoto: peitschphoto.com (Peter Peitsch)
Satz: DTP Andrea Eckhardt, Göppingen
Druck: Beltz Druckpartner GmbH & Co. KG, Hemsbach
Printed in Germany
ISBN 978-3-12-923003-9

Contents

The Author and his Times

The Author's Life and Works

Nick Hornby was born in Redhill (Surrey) on April 17th, 1957. His father was a successful businessman, Sir Derek Hornby. His parents divorced when he was 11 years old (nearly the same age as Marcus in *About a Boy*). When he began writing *About a Boy* he was the same age as the novel's other protagonist, Will Freeman.

His father often took him to watch football matches at Arsenal, the Premier League club whose stadium is in Highbury, North London, and Nick became a loyal fan of the team. He also became a fanatical reader, starting with boys' comics and progressing to whole series of books for boys. At school, his English teacher encouraged him to read the novels of British writers such as Evelyn Waugh and Kingsley Amis. After grammar school he went on to study English Literature at Cambridge University. After his graduation, he taught English at a school in Cambridge and to foreign students while writing reviews for *Time Out* (a leading guide to leisure-time activities) and the *Literary Review*.

Hornby's first book, a series of critical essays on American novelists, was published in 1992. *Fever Pitch*, his autobiographical memoir of a life devoted to Arsenal football club, was published in the same year, after having been refused by several publishers "because they said football books didn't sell". Hornby, however, knew "that if football fans are prepared to spend £25 on a duvet cover, then they might be interested in spending £14 on a hardback". *Fever Pitch* won the William Hill Sports Book of the Year Award and was adapted as both a play and a film (1997), the latter starring Colin Firth playing a schoolteacher trying to keep his romance going during Arsenal's first championship season in eighteen years. Hornby himself also made a brief appearance in the film, an experience which he enjoyed very much.

His fiction is mainly concerned with male obsessions, crises and weaknesses. His first novel, *High Fidelity* (1995), is the story of an obsessive record collector and list-maker, and was adapted as a film in 2000 starring John Cusack. For Hollywood purposes, the scene of the film was moved from London to Chicago.

Hornby's second novel, *About a Boy* (1998), focuses on the growing relationship between "thirty-something" Will Freeman and Marcus, a 12 year-old boy. A film version starring Hugh Grant appeared in 2002 (see pp. 89–94). His novel *How to Be Good* (2001) explores contemporary morals, marriage and parenthood from the woman protagonist's point of view. It won the WH

Smith Award for Fiction in 2002. His songbook *31 Songs* (2003) celebrates 31 songs which are of great significance to the author. Hornby's latest novel, *A Long Way Down*, appeared in 2005.

His colloquial style of writing has been compared to that of Martin Amis, but he himself says that he writes more like Kingsley Amis (an author of many witty novels who is also much concerned with male problems). Amis' 1950s classic, *Lucky Jim*, a parody of the life of a junior lecturer at a small provincial university, is his funniest book and one of the novels which Hornby read as a schoolboy. *Difficulties with Girls*, published in 1988, concentrates more on "male problems", which is Hornby's main concern in his writing.

Other influences on Hornby's writing are contemporary popular novelists such as Annie Tyler, Lorrie Moore, Irvine Welsh and Roddy Doyle. He appreciates these writers' "simplicity, humour, soul", and this is reflected in his own writing. He freely admits that most of his reading is American fiction. Of his own work he says: "My content is British, my style American."

People may envy Nick Hornby's success as an author in view of the simple style of his books (a typical reader's reaction is: "I could have written that!"), but a large part of his life is taken up by the needs of his autistic son Daniel. Because of the lack of suitable schools for the 76,000 autistic children in Britain and lack of support for their families, Hornby and his ex-wife Virginia Bovell helped to found a special school, TreeHouse, which takes the needs of autistic children into account.

Daniel was born in 1993 and was diagnosed as autistic at a relatively early age. Autism is a serious, life-long, neurological condition which prevents the development of communication, socialization and imagination. People with this condition have difficulties in making sense of the world, forming relationships and developing language. They cannot learn, as other kids do, by copying the behaviour of adults or other children. Autism begins at a very early age and affects four times as many boys as girls. Nobody knows what causes it, and there is no cure.

Of his own son, Hornby writes: "Daniel would cry most of the day, was hyperactive, and threw things around the room. He lost all eye contact and didn't recognize his family. When I tried to cuddle Daniel, he would bite, kick and scream."

The strain of bringing up an autistic child played a large part in the breakdown of Hornby's marriage, although he sees and talks to his ex-wife every day through their contacts with Daniel and at his school.

In 1999 Nick Hornby was awarded the E.M. Forster Award by the American Academy of Arts and Letters. He still lives in Highbury, North London, where *About a Boy* is set.

Political and Cultural Background to the Book

The 1960s Britain of Hornby's early childhood – the Britain of "Swinging London", Carnaby Street fashions, The Beatles and The Rolling Stones – underwent a revival in the mid-1990s, just at the time when *About a Boy* was being written. The catch-phrase was "Cool Britannia", a pun on the patriotic (even jingoistic) 18th-century song "Rule Britannia", in which Britain was portrayed as a warlike, victorious Top Nation.

Cool is the standard (perhaps we should use the more modern word "benchmark") by which Will Freeman measures himself at the beginning of the book. The phrase "Cool Britannia" actually originated with an ice-cream flavour (vanilla with strawberry and chocolate-covered shortbread) promoted by the company Ben and Jerry in April 1996 and adopted by the British media after the American magazine *Newsweek* declared, in November 1996, that London was the coolest capital city in the world.

When Tony Blair's Labour Party won the general election in 1997, ending 27 unbroken years of Conservative rule in Britain, New Labour wished to modernize all things British. The emphasis on Britain's traditional image, fostered by prime ministers Margaret Thatcher ("politician grannie [= grandmother] with your high ideals" of the Tears for Fears song "Sowing the Seeds of Love", 1989) and John Major ("Back to Basics"), a Britain of warm beer and cricket, the Royal Family, stately homes and tradition, was to be replaced by the New Labour image of a "Cool Britannia": a multi-ethnical society following the flow of integration into Europe leading to a New Britain after the millennium.

The "Cool Britannia" campaign was officially cancelled in November 2001 because it was completely out of touch with the actual reality of a Britain of collapsing public services, rioting football hooligans, violent racism, a disastrous Millennium Dome project and epidemics of mad-cow disease and foot-and-mouth disease which turned the idyllic, storybook countryside of travel brochures into a horror-film scenario of angry, ruined farmers, KEEP OUT notices and piles of dead animals being burnt. There was nothing *cool* about any of these aspects of Britain at the turn of the new millennium.

Just at the time when the Thatcher/Major Conservative government were trying their best to 're-invent' Britain, the women's liberation movement had already gone a long way towards re-inventing the family unit. The centuries-old image of the three-or-more-member family of father ("breadwinner"), mother ("childbearer/housekeeper") and child(ren) (next generation of the same) was being replaced by trendy "single-parenting" (usually mother and child/children). Little social stigma was attached to divorced or even unmarried mothers from the 1970s on, while increasing government financial assistance, help-groups etc. made single-parenting economically viable (perhaps even financially as profitable as working for a living) from the 1980s on.

Rachel's explanation of her uncomplicated relationship with her son Ali in the book ("I slept with his father and nine months later I gave birth", p. 207) could be taken as a fair comment on the changed morality of the 1980s. The word "couple" no longer necessarily meant 'married couple'. Partners were splitting up all the time, often at the slightest provocation, and were easy to replace. The chains of marriage which often tied two unhappy parents together for most of their lives "for the sake of the children" had long disappeared by the time *About a Boy* was written.

Will Freeman's own experiences at his first SPAT meeting seems to confirm the opinion of many emancipated women that "all men are bastards" (p. 20) in the negative, non-literal sense of the word. Ironically, Will decides to exploit this attitude in his search for new girlfriends by being less of a "bastard" than the men who have left their female partners.

London is now the most multicultural city in the world, and it is to this city that Marcus Brewer and his mother Fiona move from the quiet, provincial university city of Cambridge in the mid-1990s. No wonder, then, that Marcus has problems fitting in at his new school. Even if he had been less weird and geeky, he would have had problems.

There is a long tradition of conformity to certain standards in Britain in general and at British schools in particular. School uniform (or "dress code" as it is now called) is just one example. Only shirts/blouses, shoes and socks/stockings of certain colours were permitted at most schools, and the tradition continues even today. No concessions were made to the fashions of the times, and in the 1960s, when tight trousers were in fashion, many boys schools even prescribed a minimum width for trouser-legs.

It is easier for a pupil to "fit in" if he or she looks the same as the other pupils. Uniforms meant uniformity is the positive sense of relative anonymity. It was harder to spot obvious "outsiders" in the old days. The children of richer parents might have a new uniform every year, but kids at the same school had to wear the same clothes. There were also higher ethical and moral standards at British schools thirty years ago. Nowadays the standards are set by influences outside school: fashion, music, *coolness* etc. Peer-group pressure is a powerful influence: wear the wrong trainers and you are "mega-out".

The Dysfunctional Family of the 1990s

The relaxation of moral standards in Britain since the 1970s has not only generated a higher degree of emancipation among women. This increased female emancipation has also enabled men to avoid many of their moral and social responsibilities. The result: the collapse of the family unit described above.

Early on in the novel Hornby points out the many options open to men in the modern world of loose moral commitment and female single-parenting:

there are "men who took one look at their new child and went, men who took one look at their new [female] colleague and went, men who went for the hell of it. [...] by the time Suzie had finished her litany of treachery and deceit, he [Will] wanted to cut off his own penis with a kitchen knife." (p. 36) *About a Boy* highlights the problems faced in present-day Britain by the 'victims' of emancipation (unmarried mothers, fatherless children, selfish singles). Hornby portrays the dysfunctional family (Fiona and Marcus) and the role of the selfish loner (Will) without trying to moralize. Let us look at Fiona's and Marcus's problems first, because they represent an extreme example of the problems facing single mothers in present-day Britain:

- Mother and son are poor. Fiona has a job but her income is low (£400 a week.
- As a single mother, Fiona has serious family commitments to her son.
- They have recently moved to a new environment.
- Fiona has had several boy friends, but none of the relationships proves satisfactory.
- Fiona forces Marcus to accept her alternative lifestyle (they are vegetarians, they refuse to follow fashions like "sheep", they listen to old-fashioned music).
- Because they are "different", they make few friends.

The result of these problems is Fiona's depression, leading to her attempted suicide. Marcus desperately attempts to help his mother and ends up rejecting the dysfunctional family unit: "Two isn't enough. You need back-up" (quoted here from the filmscript; compare p. 66). For, in their own way, the dysfunctional family unit of Fiona and Marcus is just as much an "island" in the everyday London social scene as self-sufficient Will.

No Man is an Island

"We live in an island age," says Will Freeman in the film version of *About a Boy*. If we compare Will's situation with Fiona's and Marcus's, we find that in many respects his life is the complete opposite of theirs:

- He has plenty of money, which he does not have to work for.
- He has no family commitments. Both his parents are dead and he has no contact with his step-brother and step-sister.
- He is at home and quite happy in his North London environment.
- He seems quite happy with short-term sexual relationships.
- He is trendy and "cool", following fashions and able to afford to do so.
- He has plenty of acquaintances but few real friends.

Will avoids deep commitment (including love) because he is afraid that deep feelings can only lead to deep pain and disappointment. He tries to shut life out because, for him at least, life (apart from *The Will Show*, of which he is the star) means getting involved in other people's problems. He is thus an extreme example of another modern dysfunctional social unit: the uncommitted single.

The novel thus deals with present-day human and social problems which, although located in North London, are often the same in other developed countries throughout the world.

The Plot

About a Boy consists of two story lines which are presented separately at first in alternate chapters before combining into one story which is narrated from the points of view of the main protagonists of the two story lines, again in alternate chapters.

Story Line 1 – Marcus

Marcus is 12 years old. His parents split up a couple of years before the story starts, and he and his mother Fiona, a music therapist aged 38, have recently moved from Cambridge to Holloway in North London. The novel begins on the evening when Fiona and her latest boyfriend Roger split up. Indeed, the event is so fresh that the pizza ordered for Roger has not even arrived when the story begins.
Marcus is different from other kids of his age, so he has problems fitting in at his new school: like his mother, he is a vegetarian and does not wear the "right" clothes or trainers. He loses his only two friends at school, Nicky and Mark, early in the book because they do not want to be seen in his company. Although they, too, are "different", they fear that they will become victims of the bullying to which Marcus, as an absolute outsider and new arrival, is being subjected if he "hangs around" with them.
Fiona becomes depressed as a result of her situation and begins to cry a lot, even at breakfast time. Marcus realizes that he cannot help his mother and naively believes that perhaps he can find someone who can. A new partner, perhaps.
He meets Will Freeman at a picnic in Regent's Park organized by a single-parent organization called SPAT (Single Parents – Alone Together) which Will, who is neither a single parent nor even a father, has joined in order to exploit the possibilities of sex with single mothers. Fiona is not at the picnic (she is "having a rest" from her parental duties) and Marcus has gone with her friend Suzie, whom Will would like to go to bed with, and Suzie's two-year-old daughter Megan.
The picnic is a disaster. Marcus goes to feed the ducks and accidentally kills one when he throws a heavy piece of bread into the pond. Will helps to get Marcus out of trouble when a park-keeper turns up. The sense of disaster is lifted for a few seconds when Marcus thinks he sees his mother standing on the path in front of them. He turns to say something about his mother to Suzie, but when he turns back, the figure is gone.

When they return to Fiona's flat, they discover that she has tried to commit suicide.

Story Line 2 – Will

Will Freeman is 36 years old. He lives in North London and seems to have lived there all his life. He is a single and has never been married. He has no children and no desire for children, and although he has normal sexual appetites, his relationships with women are never permanent. The fact that he lives off the income from his father's hit Christmas song "Santa's Super Sleigh" and has never had a full-time job sets him apart from other trendy singles of his social status who have to work for a living. In this respect he is as different, in his own way, as Marcus is.

But unlike Marcus, Will wears the right clothes, reads the right magazines, listens to the right music and is otherwise a perfect representative of "Cool Britannia" (see p. 7). As an egocentric with no firm social commitments, he is in full control of his life. He spends his evenings with women or with undemanding male friends and divides each idle day (when others are hard at work) into twenty half-hour units (having breakfast, reading the paper, tidying the flat, watching TV), which gives his life shape but not meaning.

He meets Angie, an attractive single mother, and has a brief affair with her that provides wonderful sex and a painless ending for him when Angie decides she is not ready for a serious relationship. Will cannot believe his luck: he emerges from his selfish relationship with Angie as a "good guy" after all. It is then that he decides to exploit the sex potential of the huge army of attractive single mothers in London. But to do this he has to find them – they don't hang around bars in the evenings; they have kids to look after. So he joins SPAT and pretends to have a two-year-old son called Ned. This soon involves him in a complex web of lies which he finds increasingly difficult to handle.

He meets Marcus at the picnic in Regent's Park, and from here on (Chapter 8, p. 44) the two story lines become intertwined.

The Two Story Lines Combine

When Will, Marcus and Suzie return from the picnic, they find that Fiona has taken an overdose of tranquillizers. This is a turning point in Marcus's life. He realizes that (at least for a boy of his age) a family of two people is not big enough, and he spends several chapters trying to interest Will, whom he now visits regularly after school, in marrying Fiona. At this stage of the book, Marcus can think of no other solution to Fiona's depression and their family problems.

Fiona's attempted suicide marks a turning point for Will, too. For the first time in his life, he sees that he might be able to "do something with" two almost total strangers. He starts out by trying to help Marcus to fit in at school. He buys him expensive trainers (which are soon stolen) and realizes that what Marcus really needs is not an adult role model or father figure to guide him into adolescence but someone to teach him how to be a kid. This is something which his mother, with her vegetarian, alternative, almost hippy-like lifestyle, does not understand.

When Fiona discovers that Marcus is spending a lot of time with Will, there is a big argument during which Marcus, surprisingly, stands up for Will, saying that Will, not his mother, knows what he needs best.

Then Will and Marcus both fall in love: Will with Rachel, a single mother with a 12-year-old son called Ali (Alistair), and Marcus with a 15-year-old punk girl at his school called Ellie. Ellie and her friend Zoe "adopt" Marcus as a kind of mascot, which gives him some badly needed protection from the bullies at school. Will "adopts" Marcus to make himself more interesting to Rachel, but the first meeting of the two boys is almost a disaster. Ali (in a parody of the Oedipus complex) threatens to kill Marcus if his "dad" tries to date his mother.

Will is beginning to realize that he cannot carry on inventing children to make himself more interesting to women. He wants to be interesting in his own right. But he still refuses to tell Rachel the truth: that he has lied to her about Marcus being his son. Instead, he tries to convince her that she has somehow drawn a wrong conclusion. His attempt to explain his relationship with the 12-year-old is farcical in the extreme. At last Will begins to realize that he must change his lifestyle and show more commitment even to people like Fiona and Marcus, who are in need of help. Helping others (instead of only thinking about himself) would give a point to his life.

Although spring has come to London, Fiona's depressions begin to get worse again. Marcus is helpless. Will has a long talk with Fiona and begins to discover that he is able to help other people without always thinking of his own advantage.

Then Clive, Marcus's father, has an accident in which he breaks his collar bone. He then expresses a wish to see his son. Ellie suggests going to Cam-

bridge with Marcus, but on the day of the trip her favourite pop singer Kurt Cobain commits suicide. Ellie is devastated but sets off for Cambridge with Marcus, as arranged.
The trip is a disaster. Ellie gets off the train at Royston and smashes the window of a record shop whose owner, she thinks, is exploiting the death of her idol. So Marcus and Ellie are taken to the police station and the scene is set for a confrontation between the two children and Fiona, Clive, Clive's new girlfriend Lindsey, Ellie's mother Katrina and Will, who all hurry to Royston to "collect" Marcus and Ellie.
Will is now no longer a neutral observer but someone deeply involved in other people's lives. He has come a long way from the egocentric, shallow personality at the beginning of the book. He knows now that only deep, personal commitment can give his (or anybody's) life real meaning. He discovers what it is like to be human at last.

This novel is about the importance of human relationships. Marcus discovers early in the book that two people are not enough. Will still believes that one person (himself) is enough until he falls in love with Rachel.
At the end, Marcus has made great emotional progress. He feels safe at school thanks to his friends and fits in better thanks to Will's advice on clothes, music and hair styling. He becomes quite philosophical, and when faced with the idea that Will might marry Rachel, he says that he does not think that couples are the future: mainly because of their tendency to split up. For Marcus, plenty of people as "back-up" is the answer to the problems of living with a depressive single parent.
The more mature version of Marcus is easier for Fiona to handle. Although she feels she is losing him, she has to admit that she is less depressive and more able to cope with life.
Will has also made great emotional progress: from a cool, selfish egocentric to a warm human being who is prepared to become involved in other people and their problems even when there is "nothing in it" for him. Deep emotions like love always involve the risk of getting hurt, a risk which he had always tried to avoid but now decides to take.
On the final page – as a test of a theory he has – Will suggests a sing-song around the piano with songs from the Seventies as an alternative to a video evening. How about Joni Mitchell's song "Both Sides Now"? When Marcus shocks his mother by saying "I bloody hate Joni Mitchell" (p. 278), Will knows that Marcus will be all right. He has broken away from his mother's manipulation of his character. He is on his way to becoming "his own man".
Fiona's depression decreases as Marcus becomes more independent, and Will, by replacing sex with love and by exposing himself to the risk of getting hurt through emotional commitment, becomes a much more human person by the end of the book.

The Story

The story is set in the North London inner suburbs of Holloway and Islington between the autumn of 1993 and the spring/early summer of 1994.

Chapter One

Story line 1 – Marcus's and Fiona's situation

The novel begins dramatically enough with the question: "Have you split up now?" which 12-year-old Marcus Brewer asks his mother Fiona after she has had a big argument with her boyfriend Roger. Roger has shaken Marcus's hand, wished him luck at his new school and left even before the three large pizzas which have been ordered for their supper have arrived.

Fiona's reply: "Are you being funny?" is not an answer but another question, and indicates the problems which Marcus and, later, Will have in communicating with Fiona. Marcus is a serious boy and, as we shall see, does not know how to be "funny" in this sense.

These first two lines indicate one of the novel's main themes: the fragility of personal relationships. In the whole book we will only meet one happily-married couple with children (in Chapter 2). Every other adult is a single: unmarried, divorced or separated. We are living in a period of crisis for the family unit, a world of dysfunctional families.

In the first chapter we learn that Marcus's parents have been separated for four years. Since then his life has been subjected to many changes: after the "normal, boring" family life came a second kind of life which was "messier" with "more people and places in it: his mother's boyfriends and his dad's girlfriends; flats and houses; Cambridge and London" (p. 3). But Marcus doesn't mind the changes: "More happened, and that had to be a good thing."

They moved to London during the summer holidays and not much has happened yet, apart from Roger. They have looked around the area where they live, Holloway, which has "nice bits and ugly bits", and have talked a lot about London, but they are really waiting for their London lives to begin.

They decide to watch TV. Marcus doesn't want to watch a soap-opera because the problems in a soap-opera might remind his mother of her problems. In the end, they watch a nature film about "a fish that nobody could see *the point* of; he didn't think that would remind his mum of anything much" (p. 4; italics by P. N. Hewitt).

We will come across the question "What's the point?" in several contexts in

this novel, particularly in the sense of 'the meaning of life'. It is an important theme (see pp. 83–84).
Marcus doesn't worry about his mum having boyfriends. His main worries at present are 1) What shall we do with the spare pizza? and 2) How can I stop Mum worrying about her problems?

Chapter Two

Story line 2 – Will's situation

Will Freeman is cool. Our first glimpse of his character is provided by the coolness questionnaire in a magazine which Will is filling in. He scores sixty-six points! "He was dry ice! He was Frosty the Snowman! He would die of hypothermia!" (p. 6)
If we rephrase the questions in the coolness questionnaire slightly, adopting old-fashioned 'uncool' ethical values, we discover that Will goes in for casual sex, spends a lot of money which he does not have to earn, is rich but does not go to work, does not have many ethical beliefs, listens to the right music, goes to the right restaurants and is into soft drugs. Even if we take the remark about hypothermia (a condition which claims many lives among the old and poor in London every winter) as a joke in bad taste, there is a hint that Will's life lacks warmth and purpose – and that he realizes this. But cool is in, and Will thinks that being "men's-magazine cool" is perhaps his greatest achievement in life so far. He intends to keep the questionnaire – perhaps to justify his existence, if only to himself.
He wonders how people like himself (although he rejects the idea that anyone could really be like him) managed to survive in the days before daytime TV, videos and glossy magazines. Sixty years ago he would have had to get a job or he would have been bored to death, he thinks. Here we get the first hint that Will gets his income from something his father did, but we are not yet told what this was.
At this stage in the novel, Will does not feel that he needs a life of his own. It is more interesting to "peek over the fence at other people's lives, as lived in newspapers and *EastEnders* and films and exquisitely sad jazz or tough rap songs" (pp. 6–7).
So far the book has consisted of dialogue or the thoughts of the protagonists. Now we have the first comment by the author: "The twenty-year-old Will would have been surprised and perhaps disappointed to learn that he would reach the age of thirty-six without finding a life for himself, but the thirty-six-year-old Will wasn't particularly unhappy about it."

We then move to a completely different world: Will visits his friend John, whose wife Christine has had a baby – their second child – a week before. Will finds the untidy, grubby world of this obviously happy family (the only one in the whole book) appalling. He has deliberately postponed his visit for a week in the hope that the main topic of the conversation would not be the baby, but Will's complete lack of family feelings is reflected in his unfeeling realization that "everything came back to the sodding baby" and his comic-ironic conversation with Christine, who comes in with the baby:

> "'This is Imogen,' she said.
> 'Oh,' said Will. 'Right.' What was he supposed to say next? He knew there was something, but he couldn't [...] remember what it was. 'She's ...' No. It had gone." (p. 7)

For Will, family life is a trap, one into which his former girlfriend Jessica has fallen. He still sees Jessica for lunch sometimes. She shows him photos of her children and tells him he is "wasting his life, and he didn't know what it was like" (p. 9). But Will has no intention of finding out what it was like. John and Christine had been all right before they had started a family, but Christine's question: "Any desire for a family of your own yet?" makes Will feel physically ill. He has "no use [...] whatsoever" for John and Christine now that they have followed "the Jessica route to oblivion".

Just as he has decided that he "wouldn't be bothering with them again", they ask him if he would like to be Imogen's godfather. This irony – the contrast between Will's negative thoughts and John and Christine's positive suggestion – puts Will in an embarrassing position. He declines with thanks, saying, in response to John's disappointed suggestion that Will may have "hidden depths", "Ah, but you see I haven't. I really am this shallow." An ironic statement on Will's part because, at this stage in the book, however negative it may sound, it is absolutely true.

The chapter ends with the second author's comment:

> "A couple of weeks later Will met Angie and became a temporary stepfather for the first time. Maybe if he had swallowed his pride and his hatred of children and the family and domesticity and monogamy and early nights, he could have saved himself an awful lot of trouble." (p. 10)

This statement indicates that Will's problems will soon begin.

Chapter Three

Marcus's first two days at his new school

Marcus's first day at his new school has been so traumatic that he cannot sleep. There is no way round this problem. Not even "telling his mum what

was bothering him" (p. 11) will help. Not even changing schools would help. His basic problem, he thinks, is that he is someone who "just wasn't right for schools". He realizes he is not right for many things: he is too shy for parties, for instance. But there is no chance of staying at home and being taught by his mum – she has to go to work. And he will have to go to school. "[...] he had learnt that some hard things became softer after a very little while. [...] But this was only going to get worse." (pp. 12–13)
On the second day he gets to school early, to avoid the kids who had laughed about his "wrong trousers, [...] wrong haircut, [...] wrong shoes". This is the first mention of peer-group pressure. Marcus knows that he is "weird" and blames his mum. With the best intentions, she has imposed her vegetarianism, musical tastes and ethical ideals on her son, but she does not have to take the consequences: mobbing and bullying at school. If he wants to do things that normal kids do, he has to argue with her, and she is so good at arguing that he always loses the arguments and, paradoxically, admires her whenever she wins. At the university city of Cambridge there had been plenty of kids whose weird mums had made them "not right for school", but in London Marcus feels uncomfortable at school because he is so different.
But it is not all his mum's fault. He started singing to himself during a lesson the day before, and that was the best way to get the other kids to laugh at you! Telling the kids that you didn't realize you were singing just made you even weirder!
His nervous young English teacher is not much help, either. In order to get a literary discussion going, she asks the question: "How can we tell if people are mad?" (p. 16) to which one of the girls replies: "If they sing for no reason in class, miss." The teacher makes things worse by mentioning Marcus by name to earn herself points with the class, and Marcus hates her for it.

Chapter Four

"Will the Good Guy"

While browsing in a record shop, Will hears a woman asking for a record of Pinky and Perky (the singing cartoon piglets) for her niece. He does not see her face but thinks he recognizes the husky, sexy voice of the attractive blonde who orders a cappuccino in the café where Will is spending one of his "time units'" two days later.
His conversational opening: "I like Pinky and Perky, too" (p. 18) is a disaster almost of the same magnitude as Marcus singing in class, for she is not the same woman. Blushing with embarrassment, Will apologizes and explains the confusion, which enables him to start up a more normal conversation. Will soon has Angie's telephone number and a first date.

At their first date she tells Will about her children, and his first reaction is to drop his napkin and rush out of the restaurant, but Angie's beauty stops him. He tells her he thinks he might be "good at kids' things". He remembers John and Christine. Surely if they can do it, so can he? "Maybe he should have been working with kids all this time. Maybe this was a turning point in his life!" These are Will's thoughts, not the author's raised finger. His encounter with Angie certainly turns out to be a turning point in his life, but in quite a different way, as we shall see in Chapter 6.

But it is Angie's beauty, her similarity to the famous blond, blue-eyed actress Julie Christie – going out with a famous actress lookalike might enhance his coolness for the next questionnaire – that makes him good with Angie's kids. He decides that a beautiful single woman with a child or children is easier to pick up. Here was a "new, life-changing strategy" (p. 20) for Will's sex life. As Angie begins to quote the angry list of feminist clichés about men, Will begins to get excited. If single mothers who had been badly treated, then abandoned by their partners think that "all men are bastards", he will show them what a Good Guy he is. Then he can go out with women who looked like Julie Christie forever! So, for the next few weeks, Will the Good Guy, takes Angie and her children on excursions, treating, in his opinion, fatherhood as "a kind of sentimental photo-opportunity" (p. 21).

Will soon decides that sex with a single mother is fantastic. Tied to the home in the evenings, a single mother has few chances to meet men and appears to be so grateful when any man finds her attractive. "All of a sudden," thinks Will, "you became better-looking, a better lover, a better person." He now sees that sex between childless singles is "just another fuck". With a single mother it is more exciting. If other men might have moral objections to exploiting the emotional problems of single mothers, Will doesn't mind: it will reduce the competition.

Paradoxically, Angie does not love Will for what he is – a shallow, cool nobody – but because he is *not* like her ex-husband Simon. This makes things so easy for Will that he is almost ashamed that something so effortless should have such great rewards.

After six weeks, however, he decides to end their affair because Angie's family arrangements (babysitters arriving late, the fact that she cannot stay overnight at his place, the fact that she has neither video, nor satellite, nor cable TV) are unsatisfactory. He has never been good at ending affairs, but amazingly – and ironically – it is Angie who ends it, saying she is not ready for a new relationship yet: "The tragedy is that I've met someone just right for me at precisely the wrong time. I should have started with a meaningless fling" (p. 23). The irony here is that Will has only been *pretending* to be a good guy. For him, their relationship has *never* been more than a meaningless fling, though it is too late to tell Angie now, and telling her may lead to embarrassment and loss of face for Will, things which he wishes to avoid at all costs.

Angie begins to cry, so Will is given a rare opportunity to end a relationship without feeling guilty or responsible, even, ironically, being able to 'forgive' the woman he has actually been exploiting. There is perhaps even a trace of sadism in Will's thoughts: "Of all the evenings he had spent with Angie, he loved the last one the best." (p. 24)
Will sees the opportunity of a new career as a "serial nice guy" (*serial* is usually used in connection with repeated criminal behaviour as in 'serial killer'. But perhaps many people would consider such exploitation of single mothers as a crime, so the choice of phrase is not just humorous but ironic, too). "[...] he knew he had a lot to offer. Great sex, a lot of ego massage, temporary parenthood without tears and a guilt-free parting – what more could a man want?" Perhaps, the reader may think: love, a secure family life, building a future for the children... But the reader is not Will. "Single mothers [...] were the best invention Will had ever heard of. His career as a serial nice guy had begun." (p. 24)

Chapter Five

Depression of a single mum

"One Monday morning his mother started crying before breakfast, and it frightened him." (p. 25) Fiona is suffering from depression. Marcus does not use the medical word, but he knows something is badly wrong. Because he does not know why she is crying, he cannot help her. So he makes her a cup of tea, the traditional British method of cheering someone up.
On his way to school, he tries to work out what is wrong. They have enough money. Nobody in the family has died. "Something to do with men?" he asks himself. He knows she wants a boyfriend, but if this is the case, why did she break with Roger?
At school, his two friends Nicky and Mark – who, like Marcus, try to keep out of the way of "anybody with a big mouth and a sharp haircut" (p. 27) – tell him that they do not want to be seen with him any more because they are beginning to get involved in the bullying which Marcus gets from the older boys. All three of them wear glasses, all three are "nerdy and geeky", but Marcus has made the older boys notice the other two, and this chapter contains a typical sample of the kind of verbal aggression reserved for "weird" kids.
Marcus understands. He must keep away from them. But his position is even more hopeless now. Now he has no friends, nowhere else to go.

Chapter Six

Will becomes a father

"I'm a single father. I have a two-year-old boy," Will repeats to himself, although he does not really believe it. He is lying to himself now, not just to other people. Why? "He had run out of single mums", so he is on his way to a meeting of a single parents' group in the hope of picking up another attractive single mother.

He has 'invented' a two-year-old son called Ned in order to qualify for membership of SPAT. Will sees nothing wrong about pretending: he has pretended to be interested in doing social work, in opening a restaurant or a bookshop. So why not pretend to be a single father if it will help him to meet single mothers who look like Julie Christie?

Will arrives punctually at the meeting to find only the organizer, Frances, unpacking the drinks for the evening party. All the other single parents are probably having babysitter problems, she tells him. He invents a story about his mother looking after Ned, but is soon feeling nervous that he is showing the wrong reactions to the situation.

At last the single mothers begin to arrive, and only one of them, Suzie, seems to attract him. She is "tall, blond, pale, nervy-looking and beautiful. [...] Blond and beautiful were two of the qualities he was looking for; pale and nervy-looking were two of the qualities that gave him the right to do so," Will thinks (p. 35).

Luckily for him, Suzie does most of the talking. She tells him her story. Her husband had started an affair while she was pregnant and left the day before she went into the hospital to have her baby, Megan. He had only seen his child once, by chance, in a shop in Islington. The other women have suffered variations on the same theme: "Men who took one look at their new child and went, men who took one look at their new [female] colleague and went." (p. 36) By the time Suzie has finished telling Will about the other women "he wanted to cut off his own penis with a kitchen knife". Is this perhaps the beginning of a guilty conscience? He is happy to hear that at least one other man is a member of SPAT: Jeremy. But he was not "dumped" by his wife. She was killed in a car crash.

To redress the balance a little, Will lies about his fictitious "ex" who, he says, doesn't care whether she sees Ned or not. He even feels that his lying is becoming more like acting (self-deception here!). "He wasn't a fraud. He was Robert De Niro." He even feels tears in his eyes when he tells Suzie how brave Ned is. When she puts her hand on his arm to comfort him, he knows he has found his next 'victim'.

Chapter Seven

The woman under the coat

Marcus spends the first weekend of the school term with his father and his father's girlfriend Lindsey in Cambridge. Marcus likes Lindsey – even Fiona likes her – but he stores up stupid things which she says or does as "ammunition" to use at home with his mum.

When he goes back to school on Monday, he wonders whether he has been making a fuss about nothing. But the bullying starts again after school in a newsagent's shop where Marcus is looking at the computer magazines. The shopkeeper, Mr Patel, is an Indian and Fiona often talks to him about India, which she had visited "when she was a real hippy".

Marcus begins singing to himself in the shop, and some kids from school harass him by putting sweets into his pockets to make it look as if he has stolen them. Luckily, Mr Patel has seen them doing it, but his – and other people's – advice to keep out of their way is easier said than done.

When Marcus arrives home he finds his mum lying on the floor under a coat watching kids' cartoons on TV. She has taken the afternoon "off sick". When he asks her "What kind of sick?" (p. 40), he gets no reply because he is "only a kid". But is he? "He was having a shit time at school and a shit time at home". He cannot help himself. The only person who can help him is "the woman under the coat". He gets angry and tells her that if she cannot look after him properly, she must find someone who can. This only makes her cry, which terrifies him. He tells her she must stop. She tells him she can't. So he goes upstairs to play computer games, even though it's a "school night". This episode highlights the theme of Marcus's helplessness in the face of his family situation.

When he comes down again, Fiona has pulled herself together enough to make them some pasta, but Marcus knows that people do not stop being crazy – and he now realizes that this is "the kind of sick" Fiona is suffering from – because you tell them to stop. "[...] but he didn't care, as long as she was OK in front of him."

Fiona – her name is first mentioned here on p. 42 of the book – then tells him that he is going on a SPAT picnic on Saturday. Marcus does not like the SPAT people – except his mum's friend Suzie, who will be looking after him to give Fiona a break (from Marcus?). Most of the SPAT kids are ten years younger than him, and after a trip to the zoo with them he had told his mum he wanted a vasectomy because he did not want to have children.

Despite his protests, his mum tells him he must get out of the house and do something normal. "I just know that we're not doing each other any good." This remark hurts Marcus, who knows that his mum is not doing him any good, either. But what has he done to her? He does not ask the question, however, because he is not sure he would like the answer. And perhaps it would involve him in another of the "arguments" which he has with his mother and which he hates, because he always loses them.

Chapter Eight

The story lines come together – Dead Duck Day

This is the chapter where Marcus and Will finally meet: at Suzie's house before the SPAT picnic in Regent's Park.
Will pretends that his ex-wife has suddenly appeared and taken not only their son Ned but also Will's car. Suzie's reaction is: "What a *bitch*. [...] You'll have to toughen up." (p. 44) Despite the fact that both Ned and Paula (his "ex") have no existence outside Will's imagination, he realizes that he must show some anger so as not to appear as a "hopeless, spineless wimp" to his new prospective girlfriend. Marcus, "the strange kid they were apparently stuck with for the day" (this is Will's first impression), says nothing at the moment.
Will begins to realize how confusing his web of lies is becoming. His little play already has a cast of three, two of whom do not exist and one of whom (his babysitting mother) has long been dead. "[...] there would soon be a cast of thousands." Can he keep on acting? If he gets rid of Ned (in a tragic accident or by packing him off to Paula), "he wouldn't be a single father any more", which is the whole point of his act.
Perhaps he should just walk away, he thinks. But that is not his style. For Will has a genuine fear of embarrassment (as many people have), so he continues his playacting without realizing that any future embarrassment will be his own fault. Despite the huge potential for embarrassment if he is found out, Will accepts Suzie's offer of a coffee and discovers to his own surprise that he is "really enjoying himself".
When Suzie asks Will what he does for a living he uncharacteristically tells her the truth: "My dad wrote a song. In nineteen thirty-eight. It's a famous song, and I live off the royalties." (p. 47)
Here comes genuine embarrassment for Will, for the song is called "Santa's Super Sleigh", and Suzie and Marcus start singing it. "People always did this. [...] and they always sang the same part." Will explains that the song is on every Christmas album ever made: even Elvis sang it. Cool Will does not like any of the recordings and hates himself for making a living from an absolutely 'uncool' song sung by so many 'uncool' singers.
"But haven't you ever wanted to work?" asks Suzie, to which Will can only say that he never seems to get round to it. Every day he gets up wanting to sort out his career problem, but other things get in the way.

Anxious to impress Suzie, Will tries to talk to Marcus about football (which Marcus hates) and music (Marcus likes Joni Mitchell, which is the closest his mother has ever taken him to pop/rock), and we have the strange picture of a trendy 36-year-old "teenager" (Will) talking to a boy of 12 who is "dressed like a twenty-five-year-old chartered accountant", i.e. a serious but boring adult, "on his day off" (p. 49). The irony of the situation is emphasized by Marcus's question: "Are you getting these questions out of a book?" which makes Suzie laugh and Will blush with embarrassment.
When Will thinks that Marcus is not listening, he asks Suzie what is the matter with Marcus's mother. Suzie says she is "just a bit under the weather" but Marcus, who has heard the question, gets closer to the truth when he says "She's going nuts" in a tone of amused anger which Will remembers his father using during the last few years of his life whenever things were actually much worse than people were pretending. So even shallow Will has an idea that Marcus's and Fiona's situation is really bad.
He is surprised to see how quick Marcus discovers a person's weak spot and mercilessly exploits it. He lies to Will about the kind of music which is popular at school and almost accuses Suzie of not taking better care of his mother. Suzie, feeling guilty for no good reason, says: "I suppose I'm going to have to ring [Fiona] every day." Marcus walks on ahead of them to the SPAT picnic he is determined *not* to enjoy while Will and Suzie follow him, feeling "old and beaten and found out" (p. 51).
At the picnic Will joins in the children's games with an enthusiasm normally only produced in him by drugs or alcohol. He does anything to keep away from the other SPAT parents and Marcus, who is "throwing pieces of leftover sandwich *at* the ducks". This use of the preposition *at* instead of *to* shows that Marcus is angry: he is not *feeding* the ducks. He is trying to *hit* them.
Little Megan falls asleep. "She's beautiful," says Will, looking at the sleeping child. Suzie shows the paradox of her situation when she says: "When I see her like this, I think 'what a gorgeous baby', and then I think 'you bastard'." Actually, Megan is technically the bastard and her father, as Suzie herself says, is "gorgeous ... You end up hating your own child and loving the man who dumped her." (p. 52)
Will is beginning to feel cheap and confused, so he brings the conversation round to the topic of finding another man – perhaps a boyfriend; perhaps himself? Just as he thinks the fish is going to bite, Marcus turns up with the shattering news: "I think I've killed a duck."

Chapter Nine

The oldest 12-year-old in London

Marcus cannot believe that he has at last managed to do something he has actually been trying to do: it has never happened before. He had been trying to hit a duck with a piece of bread. He had not wanted to kill it, of course – perhaps it had been about to die from a heart attack, he thinks, hopefully. But when Will sees the size of the french loaf which Marcus has used as a missile, and when a park-keeper (presumably alerted by a bystander) accuses them of committing "a criminal offence", Marcus knows he could soon be in big trouble.

At last Will's gift for invention is put to positive use. He claims that the duck was already dead and that Marcus was just trying to sink the body because Megan (now fast asleep in her buggy) was getting upset. Marcus suddenly begins to like Will. The park-keeper gives in, and the three of them begin to walk back to the picnic.

It is then that Marcus sees – or thinks he sees – his mum, standing on the path ahead of them. He turns round to point her out to Will and Suzie, but when he turns back, the figure is gone. "He felt stupid and didn't say anything about it to anyone, ever." (p. 56)

This is the only supernatural moment in the book, and it occurs here for good reason. Because when they return to Fiona's and Marcus's flat, a new part of Marcus's life begins without any warning at all. Fiona is lying on the sofa, pale-faced. There is a pool of sick on the carpet. She has tried to commit suicide by taking an overdose of pills.

The deathly silence of the room is suddenly broken by Suzie's screaming, Megan's crying, Fiona's moaning, Will's phoning for an ambulance. Only Marcus is silent. He does not cry. This is much too serious for tears. When Suzie screams at Fiona: "You've got a kid. How could you do this?", Marcus realizes that people may even think that he is partly responsible.

Marcus has seen scenes of violence on video, but this is "the scariest thing he'd ever seen [...] and he knew the moment he walked in that it was something he'd have to think about forever." (p. 58)

Chapter Ten

An interesting evening for Will

On the way to the hospital, Will tries to comfort Marcus. "She'll be OK," he says, but Marcus replies with words which we will come across often in the book: "[...] that's not the point." The point in this case is that Fiona might try

again. Will, however, seems to be almost enjoying "the evening's entertainment", standing apart from the seriousness of a situation which has nothing to do with him.
When Suzie tells Marcus that Fiona was asking after him in the ambulance, she means to comfort him, but he shows an unexpected capacity for sarcasm by saying: "That's nice of her." (p. 60) His experience has suddenly made Marcus "the oldest twelve-year-old in the world". He looks critically at the people in the hospital waiting room – most of them "deadbeats who had transferred the chaos of their daily life from one place to another" – and says: "My mum's not like these people."
Suzie comforts him again, and Will agrees, but thinks that Fiona may still be in trouble if the only difference between her and the deadbeats is "Suzie's reassuring car keys and Will's expensive casual clothes" (p. 62). But Will buys his things for himself alone. If Fiona cannot afford such things, that's just too bad, thinks selfish Will.
Fiona must stay in hospital overnight, so Marcus goes home with Suzie, who says she hopes Will can get things sorted out with Ned and Paula. It takes Will a moment or two to remember who these two people are: "Ah, yes, his ex-wife and son" – a thought which seems to be another humorous irony on the part of the author. Will then thinks: "It had all been very interesting, but he wouldn't want to do it every night." (p. 63)

Chapter Eleven

Two people are not enough

While waiting for his mother to return from hospital the next morning, Marcus finds and reads his mother's suicide note. The words: "I'm tired and bored and the party's gone on too long and I want to go home" (p. 65) must strike him as very selfish.
Although Fiona, after coming back, says that she feels better "at the moment", Marcus realizes that the situation causing her depression has not gone away. He feels responsible towards his mother but cannot look after her all the time. His conclusion that two people are not enough (if one "dropped off the edge", you were alone) marks a turning point in his own life. He decides to do something about increasing the size of his mini-family.
They decide to watch a video and Marcus carefully tries to select one which has nothing to do with death. Unfortunately his choice turns out to be "all about suicide". After a while he switches it off and pretends to want to watch something on TV, but Fiona wants to see the rest of the film even though Marcus explains that he doesn't want her to watch a film about what she had tried to do the day before. Marcus is confused that his mother is apparently

so normal after such a momentous event as her attempted suicide. Nevertheless, he turns the video back on and they watch the rest of the film.

Chapter Twelve

Will thinks about his life

Will is proud of the fact that he can fill his days with units of activity that last half an hour. His days are sometimes so full of these essential units that he wonders how his friends can work *and* live at the same time.

He has occasionally applied for a job, but has always regarded the world of work as a "dreamy alternative reality that didn't touch his real life, whatever that was, at all" (p. 72). So he is not even sure what his "real life" is. But his dramatic encounter with Marcus and Fiona makes him think that, perhaps, he could give their lives "a bit of shape and gaiety". He phones Suzie to see if she thinks this would be a good idea. She does, and she says she can't wait to meet Ned, so deception continues.

In the meantime, Will tries to decide what a 12-year-old boy might want to do on a Saturday afternoon. Even the attractions in the trendy leisure-time magazine *Time Out* do not seem very attractive to Will. Marcus solves the problem for him by ringing Will up and agreeing to go out with him if his mother can come, too. Marcus is generous enough to invite Will to bring Ned with him. Suddenly Will realizes that if he has a two-year-old son, there ought at least to be a child's seat in the car.

He buys one and, on his way home, buys some biscuits and crisps to crumble onto the seat to make it look more genuine. This humorous episode is shown to great advantage in the film, when a surprised family catch Will dirtying the brand-new seat.

Chapter Thirteen

Marcus the Matchmaker

Marcus now concentrates on getting his mother and Will together. With Will and Ned there would be four of them, he thinks. His mum was 38, so they could have another baby. Then there would be plenty of people in the family and it would not matter if one of them died.

Marcus makes his mother change into different clothes before Will arrives to take them out for lunch so that she will look her best for the "date" he has arranged.

The original plan to eat at "Planet Hollywood" on Leicester Square (in Lon-

don's West End) is changed when they see the queue of tourists waiting outside. So they go to another less-well-known restaurant and Marcus tries to get the big romance going, quite unaware of the chemistry involved in adult love. There is something comic yet pathetic about his naivety and his desperate attempts to get his mum and Will to start up a conversation.
The theme which the three of them finally start discussing is marriage. Neither Fiona nor Will have been married, so Marcus asks why other people bother. "Security. Pressure from family. Misguided notions of romance," is Fiona's answer (p. 86), at which Will laughs and calls her a cynic. But at least the conversation has started – a conversation which again involves lies about Ned. The food arrives and Marcus begins to eat, wondering happily whether they would move into Will's place or buy somewhere new.

Chapter Fourteen

One of life's visitors

Although Will realizes that Fiona is not his type (his main criticism of her is that she does not seem to care about her appearance or the clothes she wears, once more emphasizing his own shallowness and his concentration on external values) he feels that he would like to help them. He had 'helped' Angie by sleeping with her, now he is going to find out if he can help someone *without* sleeping with them.
But after a vegetarian supper and a musical evening at Fiona's flat, he decides that this thirty-something depressive hippy and her weirdo son are beyond his help. When Fiona sits down at the piano and sings, it is her **sincerity** that embarrasses him. This is not surprising in view of his own lack of sincerity. When Fiona sings a song she really *means* it. She even closes her eyes. Marcus does the same. Will decides, again selfishly, that he had been stupid to think there was anything here for him.
Will lacks **commitment**: you have to be committed to be a vegetarian or to sing 80s songs with your eyes closed, or to be a mother for that matter. Commitment, he decides, leads to depression and suicide, whereas his commitment-free lifestyle will whiz him effortlessly to the grave after a long depression-free life. He decides that he has taken the single-mother thing as far as he wants to go, and returns to his old lifestyle, filling his "time-units" as effortlessly as before.
But then Marcus visits him one afternoon and accuses him of lying to everybody about his son Ned. He tries to "do a deal", promising not to tell anyone that Will has been lying if he goes out with his mum. Will sends Marcus home. "I'll be back," says Marcus (p. 93), and Will is worried. When he had joined SPAT he had wanted to enter the world of unmarried mums. He had

not expected one of their children to enter *his* world. He is "one of life's visitors". He doesn't want to be visited.

Chapter Fifteen

Will takes Marcus's problem seriously at last

Marcus does not tell his mother what he knows about Will. He might be able to use the information later. But he begins to visit Will after school. They watch TV. Then Marcus takes a closer look at Will's flat and the pictures of jazz musicians on the walls. He does not recognize them, but Will tells him they are cool. When Marcus asks him why they're cool, Will says: "Because they took drugs and died, probably." (p. 97) This is one aspect of coolness.
Will's kitchen is full of modern gadgets which look as though they have never been used. They begin to talk about school and Marcus explains that he is not suited to school. Both he and his mum are introverts, but knowing that does not help either of them. Will immediately realizes that Marcus is having a bad time at school and asks him about it.
Marcus visits Will frequently that autumn, and Will begins to take a serious interest in the boy. He asks how Fiona is, and whether Marcus is bothered about the thought that she might try to commit suicide again. Although Marcus says that it bothers him a bit when he thinks about it, one of the reasons why he comes round to Will's flat is to avoid going home and possibly finding her like he did on Dead Duck Day. And he thinks about it all the time. Could he tell Will that? He cannot tell his mum or Suzie or his Dad – that would upset them. All he wants is a promise that it will never happen again, and nobody can promise him that.
But when he tells Will what is worrying him, and Will reacts with the words: "Fucking hell," Marcus feels better because it means that at least one person takes his worries seriously.

Chapter Sixteen

Making Marcus invisible

Marcus's afternoon visits soon become part of Will's daily routine, and Will feels that he is serving some purpose in the boy's life, not just filling empty units of time.
Marcus's big problem at present, however, is his mother's attempted suicide and Will, who has spent all his life avoiding real situations, cannot help him. Will has little contact with the real world. His income comes indirectly from

a fantasy figure (Santa Claus) in whom the real world does not seriously believe.
Marcus talks about his father and his father's girlfriend Lindsey, but the conversation is rather one-sided. Marcus's problems are not Will's problems. In fact, Will feels that he has no problems and is pleased that he has reached the age of 36 without encountering the real problems of the world outside: marriage, work, social problems and so on.
The following week, he opens his door to find Marcus being bombarded with hard sweets by two older boys from school. Will chases them away, surprised and pleased at his unusual display of courage, and only now begins to realize the full seriousness of Marcus's position at his new school. Marcus's own apathy towards his situation is beginning to break Will's heart. This is the first sign of any strong emotional commitment by Will in an unselfish context. He wants to stop the bullying. He realizes that even such a weird outsider as Marcus has to conform a little more in order not to be an obvious victim at school. He buys Marcus a pair of Adidas trainers so that the boy will look not invisible but *less* visible. More like the "sheep" whom his mother despises but who are making her son's life so miserable.
Walking home, Will has a pleasant but unusual feeling of self-worth. He has made an unhappy boy temporarily happy with one of his rare unselfish actions. There was nothing in it for him – he hadn't even wanted to sleep with the boy's mother. The following day, however, Marcus arrives at Will's door in his socks. His Adidas basketball boots have been stolen.

Chapter Seventeen

Marcus wins his first argument

When Marcus gets home, he has to explain the theft of his shoes to his mother. She had not noticed the big white boots when Marcus had put them on that morning, but when he arrives home in his socks (Will has given him a lift), she is shocked. Marcus tells her that Will bought the expensive boots and that they have been meeting at Will's flat regularly after school most afternoons. He also tells her that Will does not have a son. Again Fiona is shocked. They go round to Will's flat for a showdown.
Surprisingly, Will shows Fiona that he knows more about what is going on than she does. This surprises Marcus, too. After the initial embarrassment of the unmasking of his SPAT intentions, Will gets very angry at Fiona's lack of understanding for Marcus's miserable life at school.
On their way home, Marcus tells his mother that only Will knows what he needs. Fiona denies this, which places Marcus in a dilemma. He can either trust his mother and put up with bullying at school because she tells him

things will turn out all right in the end (because, as his mother, an experienced adult, she can perhaps see things which he cannot), or he can decide that Fiona is a crazy, depressed, suicidal person who does not know what she is doing. In that case, he would have to be "his own mother", without any idea of how to handle future problems which he had not known about until now and still knows nothing about. A terrible dilemma for a 12-year-old! This brings him back to the same problem: there are still only *two* of them at home, and *at least* one of them is crazy.
Marcus begins to realize that he has always accepted that what his mother has told him – or told him to do – was right. He begins to think for himself (something his mother always says she has wanted him to do) and begins to question their whole lifestyle. His mother would like to think that he agreed with her own views and tastes, but Marcus realizes that he does not really agree – he has just lost the arguments they have had about these things. Fiona always wins.
Marcus realizes that he has to have more contact with other people. Suzie is too like his mother, Will is not. When Fiona asks Marcus to give her a good reason for going round to Will's place, he says that he needs a father. It is not the right reason but it shuts her up – which stops the argument – and makes her cry. Marcus is pleased, despite his mother's tears. He has won an argument for the first time in his life.

Chapter Eighteen

Shutting life out

On November 19th, Will hears the song he hates most – "Santa's Super Sleigh" – for the first time that year. Although he lives off the profits of this "one-hit wonder", he hates it because it proves how badly his father had failed as a songwriter.
Will hates Christmas, mainly for the memories of what the song had turned it into for him and his family. Now his parents are both dead, and Will's only plans for Christmas are to watch films, get drunk and get stoned. He is thus admitting that the song "Santa's Super Sleigh" sends him regularly into his own kind of depression at least once a year.
Will thinks about Marcus and realizes that their childhoods are similar in many ways. Will had worn the right clothes at school and had bullied other children to avoid being bullied himself. But his father had killed himself with drink just as Fiona had tried to kill herself with tranquillizers. Will knows that he should use his own experience of growing up with a crazy father to save Marcus from a similar fate. But he decides it is too much work.
Then Fiona rings up the next day. The conversation begins with a statement

that Marcus does not need a father – and certainly not one like Will. When Will agrees (or, alternatively, suggests that Marcus use his own father as a father figure), Fiona accuses him of wanting to push Marcus aside. Reluctantly, Will agrees to meet her for a drink to "talk face to face" about "this whole thing" (p. 128).

They meet in a quiet pub. This is the first time Will has been to a pub with a woman in whom he has no sexual interest whatsoever. Strangely enough, he becomes absorbed in their conversation. Fiona does not criticize him but talks as if they were both involved in a relationship which she cannot change. Will's entry into Marcus's life is, for her, a sign that she has failed as a feminist single parent.

Will tries to cheer her up by telling her that Marcus does not really need male company. Marcus only said what he said to win an argument with his mother – to get his own way. Fiona cannot believe this. Will sees that Fiona's vulnerability comes from her deep emotional engagement with her son, and he rejoices that he has so far avoided such emotional commitment. Loving someone is a risk Will is not prepared to take. There is too much potential for pain in deep emotion.

By agreeing to almost everything that Fiona says, Will makes it impossible for her to argue with him. This frustrates her and she begins to contradict herself. When she asks Will to control that part of Marcus's life which she cannot control, he refuses. In her frustration, she calls Will a "selfish bastard", he points out that he cannot be selfish because he is on his own. He is not putting himself first because there is nobody else.

"Well, he's [Marcus] there too now," says Fiona (p. 133). "You can't just shut life out, you know." But Will still believes he can.

Chapter Nineteen

Marcus blows his top

Marcus does not like the idea of his mum talking to Will without him. He knows now that his "happy families" plan will not work with Will.

Fiona is back home from her 'date' at five past nine and tells Marcus that she and Will have agreed that Marcus must not visit him again. Marcus is not worried. He knows how loud the front-door buzzer is in Will's flat!

The next day Marcus has to see the headmistress at school about his stolen trainers even though he knows what might happen to him if he tells her who the thieves were.

Waiting outside the office is the punk year-ten (15-year-old) girl Ellie McCrae, who is famous for being always in trouble at school. This time it is her sweatshirt with a picture of the pop singer Kurt Cobain. Ellie tells Marcus his name

is Kirk O'Bane (it is not quite clear whether Marcus simply misunderstands her) and he is a famous footballer playing for Manchester United (p. 138), thus obviously making fun of Marcus.
When Marcus is called in to see the headmistress, Mrs Morrison, only to hear once more the advice "keep out of the way" of the kids who bully him, he loses his temper and marches out of the office.
His outburst makes him feel better. Instead of "hanging on" and pretending that his problems at school were difficult but normal, he is now in free fall and decides to play truant for the rest of the afternoon, wondering if the "Mrs Morrison moment" (p. 140) will be the moment his whole life changes. Perhaps it was the same for tramps, criminals and drug addicts. One moment changes their lives. But he is not ready for such a change. He does not want to become a truant, he is just fed up with Mrs Morrison. There has to be a difference, he thinks.

Chapter Twenty

Helping Marcus to be a kid

Will is driving his car aimlessly around North London. He often does this for fun, or to hear music louder than he could in his own flat. No normal person would want to drive a car around London for fun. It is no fun. It only builds up frustration and anger in most motorists, but sometimes Will's actionless life makes him feel so fed up that he enjoys building up a little frustration and anger.
He is singing along with Kurt Cobain's punk and grunge band Nirvana, using their loud angry rock music as a replacement for real feelings, when he sees Marcus walking down the street when he should be in school. Will feels a sudden affection for this boy who is so locked into himself that he seems to want nothing and everything at the same time, but the affection is not strong enough to make him want to stop.
When Marcus rings Will's doorbell at exactly 4.15 (to make it seem that he has come straight from school), Will tries to ignore him. He puts on a Nirvana record – loud. After thirty minutes of Marcus's buzzing in time with the music, Will lets him in.
Marcus wants to ask Will a favour: to take him and a friend to a football match. Will soon discovers that Marcus's knowledge of football is limited to what Ellie has told him – all untrue – about "Kirk O'Bane", the man on her sweatshirt.Will tells Marcus that he saw him playing truant, and Marcus explains about the scene with Mrs Morrison that led to it. He asks Will to go and talk to the headmistress, but Will tells him this would not help. He is not Marcus's father. But Marcus is convinced that Will "knows things" and can help.

At last Will realizes what kind of help Marcus needs – help that his alternative single mother cannot give him: he does not need help from a father figure to become an adult or even an adolescent. He needs "help to be a kid". Will can tell him who Kurt Cobain is, for example, and this sort of information is, for a 12-year-old at a comprehensive school in London in 1993, perhaps the most important information of all.

Chapter Twenty-one

Marcus is adopted

At school next day nobody seems to know that Marcus played truant the previous afternoon. He sees Ellie and a girl from her class at breaktime and demonstrates his new knowledge about Kurt Cobain and grunge music. Will has played him a few tracks of Nirvana but he is still not sure whether he likes it.

Ellie's friend asks him his name. "Cool name," she says. Marcus is *not* a cool name, so this is obviously sarcasm again, and the girls walk off laughing, but not before Ellie's friend has said: "See you around, Marcus." (p. 149) It is the longest conversation he has had with anyone at school for weeks.

Will is sceptical when Marcus asks him if he can invite Ellie round to listen to his Nirvana records. She probably would not come and probably has a much older boyfriend. Will does not think that a two-minute conversation with a 15-year-old girl who thinks he is "funny" and who is really "taking the piss" out of him is a firm basis for friendship.

The next day Marcus talks to Ellie and her friend again. His naive questions make them laugh, and Ellie even grabs him by the neck and ruffles his hair. Mrs Morrison turns up and wants to speak to Ellie in her office about her sweatshirt. When Ellie refuses to go, Mrs Morrison asks Marcus and Ellie's friend Zoe to leave them alone while they talk. Ellie certainly has a courage which few schoolchildren have, and, when she smiles quickly at him, Marcus feels that he, Zoe and Ellie are a trio, or perhaps a triangle, with Ellie at the top and the two others at the bottom. This triangle image is perhaps a first hint of Marcus's "human pyramid" theory (see pp. 51–52).

When Ellie and Zoe come looking for Marcus in his form room, the other kids are shocked. But Marcus feels great, especially when Ellie says he is her "friend". Marcus tries to delay leaving his form room for as long as possible to enjoy this moment of notoriety. He walks across to Ellie and she plants a kiss on his head. Marcus knows she is making fun of him, but it is worth it for that kiss! When a teacher stops the trio on the way to Ellie's form room, she says they are "adopting" him. She even announces him as "the only other Kurt Cobain fan in the whole fucking school" (p. 155). When Marcus protests that he had not said he was "a fan as such" but that he thinks "they have a good beat and their [CD] cover means something", everybody laughs. Ellie and Zoe stand proudly beside their new mascot. At last someone at school has "adopted" Marcus.

Chapter Twenty-two

Happy Christmas – Will's view

As Christmas approaches, Will decides not to spend the three days of Christmas watching videos and smoking joints alone as usual. This might, he feels, send the world a message about him that he did not want to send. He wants to spend Christmas with a family: but not with Marcus and Fiona. When Marcus invites him to come over for Christmas, Will tries to refuse but ends up accepting mainly in order to avoid being rude to the boy.

Expecting the entertainment to consist mainly of Fiona's "logic-free lectures", Will is pleased to see that Marcus's dad Clive, Marcus's dad's girlfriend Lindsey and even Lindsey's mother have come. The atmosphere is friendly at first, which surprises Will after his experience of the bitter and justifiably angry atmosphere at SPAT. At first Will finds the atmosphere slightly sickening, but later, when he has drunk a little more, he begins to see that striving for pleasantness and harmony once a year is perhaps not a bad thing. And it makes Marcus happy.

Presents are distributed. Will gives Marcus a Nirvana record and a Kurt Cobain T-shirt. Fiona gives Will *The Single Parent's Handbook* as a joke. Some of the presents are inappropriate or darkly meaningful, but they all contrast with the joyless but useful presents which Fiona has given her son: a baggy, hairy pullover, a couple of books and some piano music. Marcus shows this "miserable haul" to Will with a pride that almost breaks Will's heart. Most kids of today, Will knows, would have thrown such presents back in their parents' faces and demanded a Nintendo, but Will realizes for the first time that Marcus is "a good kid" who recognizes that his mother has chosen these presents with care and given them with love.

Marcus is different from other kids. In twenty years' time, thinks Will, he will be singing with his eyes closed and swallowing bottles of pills, but at least he was kind to his mother about his Christmas presents. "Not much of a compensation for the long years ahead," thinks Will (p. 163).

Chapter Twenty-three

Happy Christmas – Marcus's view

Marcus feels that he has got the best of both worlds: useful presents from his mother and fun presents from his father. If they had still been together, Christmas would probably have been pretty boring.

The atmosphere is friendly during lunch and the early afternoon, but when Clive rolls a joint, Fiona protests, and begins to criticize his drug habit. When Lindsey asks if they can discuss the matter another time (perhaps because her mother, who does not know what is going on, is becoming interested), Fiona gets angry, saying that she can never have a conversation with Clive without Lindsey's mother being present.

Eventually Clive and Fiona agree to have a "proper conversation" (p. 166) about drugs some other time. Marcus notices that Will does not seem to be having a good time any more. The arguments have distanced him somehow from the family. It is almost as if he is laughing at them for arguing.

After supper – there are cold meats for the meat-eaters and Marcus eats some just to see the look on his mum's face – Suzie comes around with her little girl and it is their turn to laugh at Will.

Suzie's visit embarrasses Will, especially when she deliberately snubs him. Marcus is fascinated. This snubbing, Marcus decides, is one of the most exciting things he has ever seen in real life. Will goes red and obviously wants to leave, but cannot make up his mind to go.

After further embarrassments with Suzie's daughter Megan and revelations, first from Marcus that Will does nothing for a living and then from Suzie that he "pretends he has a child so he can join single parent groups and chat up single mothers" (followed by Marcus's ironic and very humorous comment that at least he "doesn't get paid for that", p. 169), Will decides to leave, held back only by Marcus's protestation that he invited Will and doesn't want him to go home yet. "All he did was make up a kid for a couple of weeks. [...] Kids at school do worse than that every day," protests Marcus. To which Fiona replies: "The point is [...] that Will left school a long time ago. He should have grown out of making people up by now." (p. 170)

Marcus continues to defend Will, telling the others what Will has done for him and saying that he is not the only one who has done something wrong. He is thinking of his mother's attempted suicide but knows he must not mention it, so he asks them the question: "[..] how come I got to know Will in the first place?" as if this were one of the mistakes they had made.

"Because you threw a bloody great baguette at a duck's head and killed it, basically," says Will. Marcus is at first horrified, but, paradoxically, Will has said the right thing. Suzie and Fiona burst out laughing and Will sits down again. The situation is saved by comedy.

Chapter Twenty-four

Will falls in love

So far we have experienced Will as a shallow, selfish individual who has his life and emotions well under control. But at a New Year's Eve party he falls in love with Rachel, a nervy, glamorous, clever illustrator of children's books, and is in danger of losing some of this self-control.

Will has never wanted to fall in love. He knows that love makes people unhappy. They lose control and cannot protect themselves. As a realist, Will is almost sure that Rachel is about to make him very miserable indeed because he has nothing that could possibly interest this intelligent, cultured, ambitious, beautiful, witty and single woman. Although Will is good-looking, educated and a good conversationalist, he feels that deep inside he is ugly and monosyllabic.

Rachel sits next to him at dinner, and for the first five minutes Will gets a glimpse of what life could be like if he were in any way interesting. He would rather not have had this glimpse.

He misses his imaginary son Ned, who had at least made him interesting as a single father. Untypically, Will does not lie about his connections with their host Robert, a TV producer. He tells Rachel that Robert used to supply him with his dope back in the 1980s. Not a very exciting connection. If anything, it makes Will appear even shallower. Rachel begins a conversation with the man sitting on her other side. How could Will win her back? The most interesting thing in his life, he realizes, is Marcus. How can he bring this weird relationship into the conversation? Politely, Rachel mentions that, to her, Nirvana sounds just like Led Zeppelin. Will seizes his chance: "I know a twelve-year-old who'd kill you for saying that." (p. 174) So, apparently, does Rachel: her son Alistair.

Instead of lying to her by saying that Marcus is his son, he simply lets Rachel believe this. Will is now being merely economical with the truth. This is at least one step towards honesty. He does not even have to lie about Marcus's mother, Fiona; "We don't live together" is the truth. Will congratulates himself on getting "the hang of this truth-telling business" – which seems to be an extremely ironic comment by the author. "Understatement" is Will's description of not actually telling the full truth.

Rachel tells him she does not live with Ali's father. As she tells Will her story, he makes sympathetic noises – something which he has had much practice with and one of the few things he is good at: listening to women talking about their problems with men.

When Rachel asks what happened between Will and Fiona, he avoids lying to her by simply saying, in desperation and confusion: "I dunno." Rachel picks up this phrase, which applies to her own relationship: "In the end, 'I dunno' is the only honest answer anyone can give, isn't it?" (p. 177)

So Will has scored again. At midnight they kiss and arrange to get their sons together soon.

Chapter Twenty-five

Marcus and Ellie

Marcus and Fiona go to Suzie's New Year's Eve party. Ellie is there, too. Her mother, a good friend of Suzie's, is dancing wildly over in a corner and Ellie seems ashamed of her, though Marcus says he thinks she looks great and is enjoying herself.

"The point is," says Ellie, "she looks like a total cretin." Here we are yet again faced by the phrase: "The point is ...". Does it mean that Marcus is wrong? Or is Ellie interpreting the situation from her own viewpoint? Her parents do not live together, either. When Marcus asks her if she minds this, she says: "No. Sometimes. Don't want to talk about it." (p. 179) This is perhaps the best summary of most modern children's confused attitude towards single parentage.

Ellie asks Marcus if he had a good 1993. The simple answer is "No", so Ellie fetches him a drink. Coke with "something in it". The "something" is fairly harmless: sherry.

Will has warned Marcus to look after his mother on New Year's Eve (presumably, Marcus thinks, because a lot of unhappy people kill themselves then), but Fiona is talking to a man he does not know and laughing a lot, so she seems to be OK. Not close to the edge of the cliff as she had been on Dead Duck Day.

Ellie tells Marcus he can talk to her about his bad year and she will understand. She has known for a long time that Fiona tried to commit suicide. Marcus has never had a proper talk with someone of his own age. Their conversation, which Marcus enjoys very much, is about a person's right to end his or her life. Marcus argues that his mother should not want to kill herself because she has to look after him. Even Ellie's argument that if Fiona committed suicide, Clive would look after Marcus sounds like an over-simplification. If his dad killed himself, Ellie says, "nobody would say [...] he's got a son to look after. But when women do it, people get all upset. It's not fair." (p. 182) Almost all kids of parents who have split up live with their mothers.

Marcus wants to keep the conversation going before Ellie wanders away to talk to somebody else. But the only thing he can think of – what boys usually say to girls at parties – is to ask her if she wants to dance. She bursts out laughing. Again Marcus has succeeded in making her laugh, which is his main function in their relationship. Ellie goes off for a smoke.

At midnight Ellie comes looking for Marcus and gives him a big hug, so he knows he has not been unforgivably stupid that evening. Then she asks him to come into the garden "to see something really disgusting".

Ellie's mum is outside kissing a man called Tim Porter, a thing that she apparently does every year. After an angry exchange between mother and daughter, Ellie and Marcus go back inside. Marcus is more shocked than Ellie by this behaviour. It would not have happened in Cambridge. Life had been simpler in Cambridge because his parents had been together and there had been "rules". There seem to be no rules in London, which makes life more complicated.

Chapter Twenty-six

Will needs Marcus's help

Will needs Marcus's help for his next meeting with Rachel, of course, so he takes him to an amusement arcade to "soften him up" and get him to agree to become his son for a while – a second Ned, but one who will actually exist and have to play a part. There is the usual nightmare conversation where Marcus "misses the point". He only seems interested in clearing up the half-truth, even offering to explain to Rachel that he is not Will's son.

Will now realizes that he is not a good liar, only an enthusiastic one. At last he tells Marcus the truth: that he would like Rachel to be his wife, the centre of his whole world. It is a great relief for Will to be able to tell somebody – even Marcus – about the woman he has been thinking about almost non-stop since New Year's Eve.

Marcus's eyes begin to shine with fascination and pleasure, for he, too, is in a girlfriend situation with Ellie. While Marcus continues shooting at monsters on the video screen, he discusses his own situation with Will. He wants Ellie to be his girlfriend, not just his friend. When he asks Will to define the difference, Will asks him if he wants to touch Ellie. Marcus asks if that is the big difference. He is not sure that he wants to touch Ellie, but he wants to be with her all the time. He wants her without Zoe – for himself. So now Will and Marcus have something in common. They have both confessed that they are in love.

Finally Marcus agrees to be Will's son for one afternoon, and Will phones Rachel to arrange a Saturday lunch date. On their way there in the car, Marcus shows a practical side to his nature by coaching Will on personal details which Will, as Marcus's father, ought to know: Marcus's weight at birth, his birthday, his favourite food etc. The conversation becomes so absurd that they both collapse into fits of giggling.

When Rachel opens the door and greets them, mistakenly calling Marcus Mark, it is Marcus who corrects her. He is not afraid of embarrassing her, and gives Will a meaningful nudge to remind him of their conversation about "misapprehensions" at the amusement arcade. Will realizes to his disap-

pointment that Rachel has not, like he has, spent the last ten days in a sleepless fever of remembering. Will has retained almost every detail of Rachel's life that she has given him, and she cannot even remember the name of Will's 'son'! This was why he was sure that falling in love was rubbish – a painful, embarrassing experience – and now it is too late.
They go upstairs to Ali's room, which – like Ali himself – has all the features of a 12-year-old stuck between boyhood and adolescence. Ali is cool, Marcus is not. It is not going to work, but Will and Rachel nevertheless leave the two boys together for a while.
Ten minutes later they hear a door slam. Rachel investigates and comes back with the alarming news that Marcus has gone home.

Chapter Twenty-seven

Ali and the Oedipus complex

Marcus tries his best, but Ali does not give him a chance. "I'll tell you, if your dad goes out with my mum you're fucking dead," is Ali's message. Marcus tries to point out that this is not really up to him. He tells Ali that Will is "pretty keen" on Rachel and that she may be keen on him, at which Ali screams: "SHE'S NOT KEEN ON HIM! SHE'S ONLY KEEN ON ME!" (p. 198) Faced with the possibility of death or worse, Marcus can either go downstairs and explain that Ali is psychotic or go home. He chooses to go home.
Will finds him at a bus stop – on the wrong side of the street – and takes him back. Marcus does not want to go back at first, but when Will tells him that Ali is crying his eyes out now, he begins to sound less dangerous. Running away was the best thing Marcus could have done.
Ali apologizes to Marcus and they shake hands, even though Marcus – naively but humorously – cannot see how Ali could have threatened to kill him "by mistake".
Rachel begins to explain that Ali had not got on with her last boyfriend. Will smiles, and Marcus observes an unusual softness in Will's eyes that Marcus sees would really work on a woman. He decides to try it out on Ellie.
Now thoroughly embarrassed by all this talk of past relationships, Rachel blames Ali for having made her talk about it. "It's OK," says Marcus with more innocent naivety. "He [Will] really fancies you. He told me." (p. 201)

Walking home from school with Ellie and Zoe, Marcus finds it difficult to practise looking at Ellie in the way Will had looked at Rachel because they never sit down and face each other. How can he gaze into her eyes if all he sees is her ears? And his thick glasses are no help in focusing.
They go into a newsagent's to buy sweets, but this is apparently one of those

'anti-kid' shops which will not allow more than three children in the shop at one time, so despite Ellie's protests that the shopkeeper is unfairly treating all kids as potential thieves, Marcus goes outside to wait. He looks at the cards in the shop window advertising items for sale or services offered, and some boys from his school come up to him and begin to bully him. Ellie comes out of the shop and begins to bully the bullies. Marcus is full of admiration for her. "Boys are peculiar creatures," she says. "Not you, though, Marcus. Well, you're peculiar, but in a different way." (p. 203)

Chapter Twenty-eight

Lying is a very short-term strategy, but Will still finds it hard to tell the truth

Will is worried because Marcus seems to be more in love with Ellie than ever. He tries to explain that the relationship looks more like pet and owner than boyfriend and girlfriend, but Marcus does not mind. He just wants to be with Ellie. His sincerity and lack of self-pity almost make Will want to hug him. Sincerity – in view of Will's previous lack of it – is a key word in this book. Will considers the difference between Marcus's simple, decent desire for Ellie and his own desire (neither simple nor decent) for Rachel.

Ellie knows who the real Marcus is: the weird boy with thick glasses who is being bullied. The Will who came to lunch at Rachel's with his 12-year-old 'son' is not the real Will. One day, Will thinks, he will learn the lesson that lying about his identity is a very "short-term strategy".

During his first dinner date with Rachel, Will decides to "correct any erroneous impressions" he might have given her. But trying to do so without actually telling the truth (Will's usual method) involves them in a comic conversation about his actual relationship to Marcus. He is not Marcus's natural father: OK so far. And he does not live with him. Will fails completely to explain his relationship to Marcus. He fears embarrassment if he tells her all about the SPAT episode. Rachel describes her own uncomplicated relationship to Ali: "I slept with his father and nine months later I gave birth" (p. 207). The simplicity of this contrasts with Will's convoluted attempts to explain things. When Rachel asks him if he has ever lived with Marcus's mother, he asks her to "define 'live with'."

The farcical conversation continues. For a while, Will even uses eating as an excuse for not speaking, hoping desperately that Rachel will change the subject. But she does not. She just waits for him to finish his mouthful before reminding him of her question.

Will then tries to convince Rachel that it was she who chose to believe that Marcus was his son. The fact that he took Marcus along to meet her in the role of his son escapes Will for the moment. Rachel's comments are ironic, not sarcastic: "It's me who's the fantasist"; "I just made it up. I thought: Cute guy, if only he had a kid, a geeky son [...] and then you turned up at my house with Marcus and [...] I made this crazy link because of some deep psychological need in me." Will completely fails to detect her irony and flounders on by telling her not to be too hard on herself.

Trying desperately to rescue a potentially disastrous evening, he goes on to tell her about how he met Marcus – without mentioning SPAT. He does not want her to think that he has a problem (but of course he has). So Rachel, expressing nothing but quiet amusement and baffled tolerance, puts her finger firmly on Will's problem: "Why did you think Marcus would make you more interesting?" (p. 209) Will does not reply to the question but asks Rachel if Marcus really had made him more interesting. Rachel is honest with him. Until he had mentioned Marcus, Will had appeared to her as a blank. No job, no passionate interests, not much conversation... Even though Marcus is not Will's son, Rachel points out, Will is involved and cares about the boy. He has not invented him (as he invented Ned, if only Rachel knew it!).

What Rachel says is intended to comfort Will, but it makes him realize that he now wants his own life and to be interesting in his own right. He has wasted his thirty-six years by failing to do this. The problem with the people at SPAT, he realizes, is not that they have kids but that they had fallen in love and made themselves vulnerable.

Now he had done the same. Soon he will, he thinks, be singing with his eyes shut, like Fiona and Marcus, and there is nothing he can do about it.

Chapter Twenty-nine

Fiona starts crying again

During the next three or four weeks nothing much happens to Marcus. Will buys him some new glasses and takes him to have his hair cut. Marcus discovers, through Will, a couple of pop singers he likes and whom Ellie does not hate. He feels that he is changing.

And then his mum starts crying again. When she starts crying at breakfast time, Marcus knows that things are serious, but now he has at least two friends he can talk to about it.

He tells Will, and Will asks him what he is going to do. Marcus has not thought that *he* would have to do anything (he had done nothing before, but Dead Duck Day had shown him that this was perhaps a mistake). He had thought that Will might "take over".

Will tries to explain that although he is Marcus's friend, he cannot do anything about his mum. He summarizes this friendship with the words: "I can tell you who Kurt Cobain is and what trainers to get, and that's it. Understood?" (p. 215) It is the way Will says "Understood?" that makes Marcus wonder whether Will really is his friend. This is the sort of thing that parents or teachers say.

Of his two friends, Marcus prefers Ellie to Will at this stage in the story. He is in love with her, and she is nice to him, whereas Will is not always pleased to see him if he calls round four or five times in a row.
Today at breaktime, however, Ellie is unhappy and worried because Kurt Cobain has tried to kill himself. He is apparently OK, but, as Ellie says: "He wants to die. It wasn't a cry for help. He hates this world." (p. 217)
Marcus feels sick. He is probably thinking about his own mother's attempted suicide, which – unlike Kurt Cobain's – might indeed have been a cry for help. He tells Ellie that Kurt Cobain is not a real person: "He's just a singer. He's just someone on a sweatshirt. It's not like he's anyone's mum." But, as Ellie points out, he has a beautiful daughter, Frances Bean, yet he still wants to die.
Marcus skips the next couple of lessons. He locks himself in the boys' toilets to think. Ellie finds him there and, remembering Fiona's attempted suicide, tries to comfort him. She surprises Marcus by saying that he knows things that she does not: about suicide, and about being Marcus, which she thinks must be "pretty scary".
To his embarrassment, Marcus begins to cry quietly. Ellie puts her arm around him and, instead of talking about something else, they sit on the pipes of the central heating until they feel like going "back out into the world".

Chapter Thirty

Sprinkling salt on the ice: Will's crisis

Will is going through the worst crisis in his life since his ex-girlfriend Jessica left him. She had told him that "he was useless, worthless, that he would never be or do anything, that he had had the chance with her to […] *sprinkle some salt on the ice* […] by having a relationship that meant something and maybe a family." (p. 220)
He knows that he should get involved with Fiona – Marcus's big problem – and look after the boy. But he does not want to get involved in Fiona's depression or in talking to her about it, because the two words he fears most are: "the point". What's the point? He knows that you cannot have a talk about life – or about ending life – without bringing up "the fucking point".
Will's life, of course, has little point at the moment. But to tell Fiona that life has no point would be the same as killing her. The only point of Will's life so far is to keep his head above water. People with reasons to live – jobs,

relationships, pets – are not in danger of being pulled down below the water. Because their lives have a point. Will wants to avoid being pulled under by a dead weight like Fiona. Rachel can keep him afloat, so he goes to see her.

His relationship with Rachel is weird so far. They have not had sex yet but she seems to like him and he certainly likes her. They treat each other as friends, but Will has a strange desire to kiss her whenever she says something interesting which, paradoxically, distracts him so much that she sometimes thinks she is boring him. The desire to kiss her would also stop the conversation that is so interesting: a double paradox! Will realizes that he has never had any kind of relationship with a woman he has not wanted to sleep with. How long can this go on? he wonders.

Then one evening it happens, without any apparent reason except that Ali is sleeping over at a school-friend's house. Will starts the evening by immediately talking to Rachel about "Marcus and Fiona and the point". Rachel sees the point as the fact that Marcus adores Will, something which had never occurred to Will before and which changes his attitude towards their relationship. Rachel has seen something which Will could not see. At first he refuses to accept that deep relationships are "the point": "If I were about to stick my head in the gas oven, and then you told me Marcus adored me, I wouldn't necessarily take it out again." (p. 225)

Rachel laughs, mainly at the idea that she would be there to mention the fact. "If you ended up sticking your head in a gas oven at the end of an evening, we'd have to come to the conclusion that the evening hadn't been a raging success." To which Will replies that he would never stick his head in a gas oven after an evening with her.

Rachel collapses into near-hysterical laughter: "That is ... the ... most ... romantic ... thing ... anyone's ever said to me!" Strangely enough, the atmosphere seems warmer when she has finished laughing. They are less nervous with each other. Rachel tells Will that he does not need "a point". She thinks he must be fairly tough to do what he does: nothing. "Most of us," she goes on, "think that the point is something to do with work, or kids, or family, or whatever. [...] There's nothing between you and despair. [...] The point is you keep going. You want to. So all the things that make you want to are the point. [...] You love things. Telly. Music. Food. [...] Women, probably." (p. 226) It is the same with her, she says, only she loves different things: poetry, paintings, her work, men, and sex, her friends, Ali...

Rachel admits that she felt really down a few years back – suicidal even – but that she always had things to look forward to. Things she did not want to miss. Although Fiona obviously has things which she should not want to miss, she is not "getting the breaks" which people need in her situation.

Rachel's simple positivism about "the point" creates a point of its own, because it is then that Will and Rachel start kissing and end up in bed at last. Half an hour in bed with Rachel convinces Will that sex is not, as he had

always thought, just a fantastic physical alternative to drink, drugs and a great night out.
Rachel suddenly suggests that she should talk to Fiona. Not knowing her might even help, and she thinks that she can show Will how to say the right things. Will does not want to think about Fiona at that moment. He cannot ever remember feeling so happy.

Chapter Thirty-one

Clive's "big think" about life

Spring has come to London. As Marcus walks home in the late afternoon sunshine it is easy to believe that his mum will get better and that life at school will improve. When he gets home, his mother seems less depressed. Fiona tells him that Clive wants to see him. Clive has fallen off a window-ledge and broken his collar bone. No wonder his mum has cheered up, thinks Marcus. Fiona thinks that Clive wants to see Marcus because he is having "this big think about life". Marcus does not want to go to Cambridge. Over the last year almost everyone he knows has been having "big thinks". His mum does nothing else all the time. Why hasn't his father had a big think before, when he wasn't falling off a window-ledge? thinks Marcus. Clive had not thought about Marcus on the hundreds of days when his collar bone was all right. Why is Clive so desperate to see his son now?
At school the following day, however, Ellie convinces Marcus that he should go and see his father. She even offers to go with him and tell his dad what she thinks of him. Marcus likes the idea of spending an hour on the train alone with Ellie and then letting her loose on his dad. She is like a guided missile in school and would presumably also "blow up" his dad if Marcus pointed her in Clive's direction. He would also be able to separate Ellie from Zoe at last. It would be like a proper date with a girl. They agree to go to Cambridge during the Easter holidays the following week.
Fiona wants to go to King's Cross Station with Marcus, but he makes her say goodbye to him at Holloway Road underground station, where she gives him a long embarrassing and melodramatic hug while all the passers-by are watching.
On the train he sees the newspaper headlines: ROCK STAR COBAIN DEAD. Kurt Cobain, aged 27, has shot himself. Marcus wonders if Ellie knows and, if not, how she will react when she finds out. Then he wonders if Fiona is OK. Her only connection with Kurt Cobain is depression and potential suicide, but the newspaper headline has somehow turned Cobain into a "real person", too. Then a feeling of sadness for all those involved, including little Frances Bean, overcomes him.

At King's Cross, Ellie is waiting for him. She seems OK. Perhaps she has not heard the news yet, and Marcus's main worry is that she will see Cobain's picture on one of the newspapers that almost everybody at the station is carrying. They have to walk to a different part of the big station, and Marcus has a great idea about how to stop Ellie seeing the newspaper headlines. He gets her to close her eyes and hang onto his jacket while he leads her to the platform. "I'm going to guide you through all these people," he tells her importantly, "[...], and then you'll trust me for ever." "If I trust you forever, it won't be because I spent five minutes wandering around King's Cross station with my eyes closed," says realistic Ellie (p. 237).
Marcus enjoys looking after Ellie. He has never looked after anything or anybody in his whole life before. He has never had a pet because he is not bothered about animals, even though he and his mum have agreed not to eat them. As Marcus leads Ellie onto the platform with the Cambridge train, Ellie suddenly tells him that she knows why he is doing this. Her voice is small and quiet. She has seen the news in the papers.
"Are you OK?" asks Marcus. Ellie says she is, but that she's going to get drunk (she has a bottle of vodka in her bag), and Marcus sees a problem with his "guided-missile plan". You cannot really 'guide' Ellie. At school there were rules and walls which she could bounce off, but out in the world there were no walls and rules. She is scary. She could just explode in his face at any time.

Chapter Thirty-two

Will learns how to listen

Will plans to bring Fiona and Rachel together for a talk at a pub. He will introduce the women to each other, then leave them to talk. He does not plan to get involved. This is to be a normal social occasion where nothing can possibly go wrong, thinks Will.
When Fiona arrives she is "distracted and slightly manic". She orders a straight gin and ice, sipping it nervously and quickly. Fiona asks Will who Rachel is and whether she herself will be invited to meet all Will's friends over a drink even though she hardly knows Will himself. The situation is becoming embarrassing.
When Rachel is half an hour late, Will phones her and gets the answerphone. He slowly realizes with growing panic that Rachel never intended to come. When he returns to his seat, Fiona is quietly crying. Will tries to ignore her but knows that ignoring her is not an option if he is worth anything at all.
"What's the matter?" he asks, but it sounds, at least to him, as if he is annoyed with her, not trying to be sympathetic. His diagnosis: "Existential de-

spair, right?" (p. 241) is correct but sounds like a shallow statement. He is just no good at chats about existential despair. Depressive hippy-liberal women are not his style. He does not think it makes him a bad person. Even his attempt at a joke falls flat.

But Fiona obviously needs to talk to someone, so they move on to a pizzeria. The Pizza Express where he used to have lunch with his ex-girlfriend Jessica, who had been determined to make him as unhappy and sleepless and burdened by parenthood as she had become, is hardly a good place to go. Will suddenly realizes that in the old days nobody's problem was his problem. Now everybody's problem is his problem and he has no solution to any of them.

Fiona tells him that all men have the same problem: unless they have an answer, they do not think it is worth bothering with the problem. This is exactly what Will thinks. But Fiona tells him that she knows he can't do anything about it. She just needs to talk.

And she talks. It was easier than Will could have imagined. He listens and nods and asks the right questions just as he has done so many times with women he has wanted to sleep with. The technique is the same, only this time there is no ulterior motive – nothing in it for him: but it will make Fiona feel better. Will is at last learning how to be unselfish.

Fiona tells Will a lot about her past: she never really wanted to be a mother even. But the sum of her depression is much greater than its causes. Depression is an illness which she has to live with. She sees everything through a greeny-brown gauze and the seat of the illness seems to be her throat: depression stops her from eating and makes her feel she is about to cry – if she is not crying already. So her depression is not caused by some great catastrophe that Will could do something about, but by Fiona's own life with its small disappointments, compromises and defeats. The resultant depression is much bigger than its components, however.

In the taxi back to Fiona's place they hear about Kurt Cobain's suicide. Will is neither surprised nor shocked, but he worries about how Marcus will feel about it, so he goes in with Fiona to listen to the answerphone message even though Fiona is sure he will be OK. But he is not OK. The call is from the police station in Royston, halfway to Cambridge. And Marcus sounds small and frightened and lonely.

Chapter Thirty-three

Unlike Marcus, Ellie enjoys her "shit life"

On the train to Cambridge, Marcus at last realizes that he does not want Ellie to be his girlfriend. She is drinking vodka from the bottle, swearing at other passengers, threatening to stop the train and is angry at the people who stare at her. His mum has told him that people sometimes need opposites, but it is not much fun being the opposite of Ellie outside school. Out in the world it is only scary and embarrassing.

Ellie is angry about the death of a person whom she loved and who understood her because of what he sang about. Ellie says that life is "shit", but Marcus realizes that Ellie *wants* life to be shit. She makes things difficult for herself, whereas Marcus's life *is* shit and he would do anything to be a normal kid like Ellie.

Ellie reminds him of Will: if either of them had real trouble in their lives they wouldn't want or need to invent it for themselves. She goes on to say that life is shit because the world is sexist and racist and full of injustice. Marcus knows this, but this is not what makes Ellie angry.

When Ellie says she sometimes feels like shooting herself, Marcus tells her that she does not feel like his mum or Kurt Cobain. She does not have a shit time, *he and his mum* have a shit time! Ellie shakes her head and laughs her "nobody-understands-me laugh", but Marcus understands her much better than last time he had heard that laugh – outside Mrs Morrison's office.

When the train stops at Royston, Ellie suddenly gets out and Marcus follows. She no longer wants to go to Cambridge. They come to a record shop in the High Street with a big cardboard cut-out of Kurt Cobain in the window. Claiming that the shopkeeper is making money out of the pop star's death already, Ellie breaks the window and takes the cardboard cut-out out of the shop front. She sits down on the pavement, hugging the cut-out close to her.

Once again, Ellie has brought trouble upon herself – as if there were not enough trouble in the world already without inventing it, Marcus thinks.

In the police car, Marcus remembers the day he played truant and the future he had predicted for himself: he was a criminal now and it was all his mum's fault because she had complained to Mrs Morrison and he had met Ellie outside her office. The point is, he thinks, that once you become a truant, you start hanging out with people like Ellie and end up being arrested.

The police are nice about the incident. Ellie explains that she is simply making a protest about the commercial exploitation of Kurt Cobain's death, which is her right as a citizen. The policemen in the car just laugh, and when Ellie gets angry and says they are patronizing her, they laugh a bit more.

At the police station, Marcus tries to explain what he and Ellie are doing in Royston, but his story only confuses the policewoman there. She says she has to call their parents.

Clive and Lindsey arrive first. Lindsey is tired and nervy because she has had to drive, and Clive is grumpy and in pain. He does not look like a man who has had a big think. He is angry with Marcus, not happy to see him. Ellie tells Clive that Marcus was trying to help her. Clive asks her who she is and what she is doing messing around with his son. Ellie says she is not messing

around with Marcus. She has come with him because he was not looking forward to a heart-to-heart talk with a father who does not understand him and who left him at a time when he was needed most. "Great, aren't they, men?" is Ellie's comment. "You've got a mother who wants to top herself and they're not interested. But they fall off a fucking window-sill and suddenly you're summoned for a talk about the meaning of life." (p. 254) Luckily, Marcus pretends that it is Ellie's mum who wants to kill herself, and Ellie takes the hint and says no more.
Clive says that Marcus probably thinks he would not have "gone off the rails" if he and Fiona had not split up, but Marcus gets angry – a rare anger that gives him the strength to argue with anyone of any age (he wishes he could buy this "anger juice" in bottles and keep it in his desk at school). He says he has done nothing. Ellie is the one who is "off the rails". She broke the window. She is his friend and he only wanted to help her. He would have done this whether his mum and dad had been together or not. "I suppose you are a useless father," Marcus goes on, "and that doesn't help a kid very much, but you'd have been a useless father wherever you were living." (p. 255) When Lindsey, who has done nothing wrong, says: "You poor kid", Marcus even tells her to shut up. But it is the "anger juice" speaking here.
Now they have to wait for Ellie's mum and Fiona, who are coming up in Will's car. The four of them sit there like actors waiting for the next scene in a never-ending play.

Chapter Thirty-four

Looking for someone less different

Will finally decides that life – in this case other people's lives – is like air: you cannot keep it out. But it is air full of bits that almost choke you when you breathe it.
He rings Rachel again from Fiona's flat. This time she is at home and confesses that she had not intended to come to the pub that evening. She thought it would do Will some good to discuss alone with Fiona, and Will admits that it did. But in future she promises to keep her appointments.
As Will sits in the car outside Ellie's house, waiting for her mother Katrina, he is reminded of Dead Duck Day. He has the same sense of chaos. The difference is that he is now not a neutral observer but somebody deeply involved in the people concerned.

Katrina is an attractive woman in her early forties. Although she admits that Ellie is "out of control", she says that she had once hoped her daughter would turn out as she has: rebellious, loud and bright. But now Katrina would give

anything for Ellie to be mousy and home every night. “She’s killing me,” she says, and Will looks at Fiona. Their children would go on killing them for years and years, always being given one more “last chance”.
Parents, Will decides, are “the Undead”. They cannot live properly and cannot die. All they can do is sit in a stranger’s car and laugh about their situation. Will wonders what Jessica means when she says he is missing out on parenthood.
They stop for petrol and to buy refreshments. When they get back into the car, the atmosphere has changed. It is a mixture of despair, shared concern, suppressed hysteria and team spirit. And Will is suddenly part of it. He finds it ironic that Marcus should be able to create such connections yet remain unconnected and lonely himself.
They talk about Kurt Cobain’s suicide and the way his fans are expressing their grief. Will doubts whether Marcus could have understood the rage and pain when listening to the music of Nirvana which Will himself had felt when listening to similar music years before. But Marcus and Kurt Cobain obviously share the ability to bring people together, which proves to Will that things are not as bad as he had thought. If only he could prove this to Marcus – or anyone.
As they get closer to Royston, Katrina continues chatting, resigned to the fact that Ellie is in trouble again, but Fiona becomes strangely quiet, and this worries Will.
The atmosphere in the police station is bad, not at the front desk but in the waiting-room. There is anger in the air. Clive accuses Ellie of acting in an insulting and aggressive way and tells Fiona that ‘her’ son is mixing with the wrong people. Lindsey complains that Marcus told her to shut up. The policewoman present is obviously enjoying the disharmony.
They are waiting for the owner of the record shop – an experiment in criminal and victim confrontation. The owner, Ruth, turns out to be a nervous young woman wearing a Kurt Cobain sweatshirt. She looks exactly like an older version of Ellie. Far from exploiting Cobain’s death, Ruth is his greatest fan in Hertfordshire and this is the saddest day in her life. For once, Ellie has nothing to say except: “I’m sorry.” Ruth opens her arms and Ellie walks over and hugs her.
This should have been the end of the cardboard cut-out Cobain episode, but Fiona’s quiet behaviour so far was merely a preparation for action. She launches into a passionate appeal to the policewoman (also a mother) for a chance for her son that will allow her to be a better mother, ignoring Marcus’s protests that he has done nothing wrong. Will is impressed: once Fiona decides to fight for her child she is unstoppable. However crazy the situation, she knows that she has to do something for her son. She tries to “do a deal” (American-style) with the police: Marcus will testify against Ellie if they let him go.

Dramatically (almost theatrically) Fiona buries her head in Marcus's neck, but he shakes her off and moves towards Will. Katrina, who has been trying hard not to laugh, goes over to comfort Fiona. "Shut up, Mum. You're mad," says Marcus with real feeling. "Bloody hell, I can't believe how crap my parents are." (p. 264)
This is a "mystical moment" for Will. He feels very peculiar. Being caught up in this messy, chaotic web of relationships between people he hardly knows shows him what it is like to be human. Not too bad, really. He decides that he would not mind being human on a full-time basis.
They all go to a burger bar for supper. Marcus again states that Ellie is not right for him. He says he should perhaps look for someone less different from him. Without realizing it, he has stumbled on the real problem of adult partnership: finding somebody who is less different. "Well, good luck," says Katrina. "There are a lot of us who've spent half our lives looking for someone less different from us, and we haven't found them so far. [...] Why do you think we're all single?" (p. 265) "It's the hardest thing in the world," says Fiona.
Will wonders if that is what they are all doing, looking for someone less different. He thinks about Rachel: she is dynamic and thoughtful and focused and caring (the exact opposite of Will, in fact). Will realizes that looking for someone less different only works if you are convinced that being you is not so bad and you do not want to change. And at this moment he realizes that being Will Freeman is not such a big deal. He will have to change a lot if he wants to become "less different" than Rachel.

Chapter Thirty-five

Marcus's "human pyramid" theory

Marcus goes to stay with his dad and Lindsey at Cambridge mainly because he feels sorry for them. He has noticed the difference between people who live in London and those who do not: the ones who do not just seem more scared of everything. Or perhaps it is the kind of people he knows now. Marcus seems to have got a lot older in the past months and he does not see what his father can offer him now, which is why he feels sorry for him.
On the drive to Cambridge, Clive moans a lot about Marcus's behaviour, but Marcus says nothing and in the end Clive runs out of moans. He cannot be "that kind of dad" any more. He has missed his moment to be a moaning parent. It is too late to worry about little things like Ellie and her behaviour. Marcus and his mum can handle these little things now, Clive cannot. Marcus judges his own recent development by the fact that he would never have been able to get arrested when he first arrived in London. He would not have known "the right people".

When they reach Clive and Lindsey's house, they have a cup of tea and Lindsey leaves Clive to have his "talk" with Marcus. Clive asks if he can roll a joint and asks Marcus to get his "tin". Marcus finds the tin in its old hiding place surprised that he can know little things like this about someone without knowing what they are thinking from one week to the next.

Clive has indeed "had a big think" since his "accident", which Marcus loves to refer to as "when you fell off the window-ledge" because it sounds less pompous and so daft. Clive says his accident has frightened him. He says that he can see now that Marcus – like every child – needs a father. Marcus replies that children need a father "to start them off", but that he is getting on OK without one now. He has had a difficult start at school but he feels safer now that he knows more people. For Marcus, these people are as important as parents. Marcus compares himself to someone at the top of a human pyramid: "You can't stand on top of your mum and dad if they're going to mess around and wander off and get depressed." (p. 271) This is a realistic statement about – and a deep criticism of – today's "partner-mobile" parents.

Clive says that his big think has been about the fact that he shouldn't have wandered off. But Marcus says this does not matter. He knows where his dad is if things get bad. And he has other people he can turn to. He says he will be all right. He will be able to cope better than Ellie (who does not think about things hard enough) and his mum (who is not very strong), and he will be OK at school because he knows who he can and cannot trust, and can create little patterns of people in a way that would not have been possible if his parents had not split up and if they had stayed in Cambridge.

This does not work for "mad" people or people who do not know anybody or for sick people or alcoholics, but it will work for him in a better way than the way his dad wants him to try (though this "way" is not mentioned in detail in the book – perhaps Clive wants him to move back to Cambridge).

They talk about Lindsey and how she wants a baby, and how his dad cannot decide. Marcus says he would not mind. He does not really like babies but he knows the value of extra people around him!

Marcus goes back to London the next day, certain that he is right about his "human pyramid" model for living. Even if it is wrong, it will help him get through life until he is old enough to make the mistakes which all the adults around him are making.

Chapter Thirty-six

Will's final dilemma

Wanting Rachel so much still frightens Will. She might change her mind about him, or find someone new, or die, even. Will feels unprotected. He does not know what this fear is all about, but he knows that it is too late to go back. That part of his life is over.

Most Saturdays, Will takes Marcus and Ali out. Visits to the British Museum and the National Gallery are not a success. All three of them are bored. But cinema visits combined with trips to McDonald's or Burger King are a great success.

Marcus is 'older' than Ali now. He dresses better and has his hair cut regularly, and his continued friendship with Ellie and Zoe has made him more teenage in his attitude. The old Marcus is disappearing.

When Ali asks Will whether he is going to marry Rachel, Will replies: "I dunno." What right has he got to ask her? He does not want to upset their relationship. She might say "no".

Marcus tells Ali that he once wanted Will to marry his mum because he thought it would sort everything out. But he sees now that this would not have been the right way. Rachel is more balanced than Fiona.

Marcus mentions his "human pyramid" theory: "You're safer as a kid if everyone's friends. When people pair off [...]. It's more insecure. [...] If your mum and Will get together, you think you're safe, but you're not, because they'll split up, or Will will go mad or something." (p. 276) "What if Rachel and I don't split up?" asks Will. "Fine. Great. Prove it. I just don't think couples are the future."

When Will tells Marcus not to patronize him, Marcus has to ask what this word means. Ironically, 36-year-old Will is being patronized ("treated like an idiot", as Will explains) by a 12-year-old who does not even know the meaning of the word. He looks at Will "as if to say: 'How else can I treat you?'" And because Will admits to himself that Marcus is probably right, he decides not to argue with him. He has no arguments to offer anyway, wishing only to save the tiny bit of "face" – dignity – which is all that is left to him.

Even Fiona realizes that Marcus seems much older now, and she is worried about losing him. She even thinks that he has been smoking. Will sees this as a positive sign that Marcus has become less geeky and more normal: "How much would you have given for Marcus to be caught smoking with his mates a few months ago?" The anti-smoker Fiona still protests, and Will decides not to press the point. But Fiona shows that she has noticed a difference in herself, too. She feels less worn down and more in control of things.

Will knows why: this version of Marcus is easier for his mother to handle. He has friends and can look after himself. He has developed the protective skin which Will has just lost. All three have had to lose things in order to gain other things: Will has lost his shell and his cool and his distance. He feels scared and vulnerable, but he has Rachel. Fiona has lost a lot of Marcus but is less suicidal as a result. Marcus has lost the old Marcus and can walk home without having his shoes stolen.

Marcus comes downstairs, bored, and asks if he can hire a video. Will wants to test his theory and suggests a sing-song at the piano with Joni Mitchell's "Both Sides Now" instead. Marcus begs his mum not to do this.

"Don't be silly," says Fiona. "You love singing. You love Joni Mitchell." "I don't. Not any more. I bloody hate Joni Mitchell." (p. 278) Will now knows at last that Marcus will be OK.

Analysis and Interpretation

1. Setting

1.1 Place

The action of the novel takes place in North London in the inner suburbs of Holloway and Highbury. Towards the end of the book there is an excursion to Cambridge, Marcus's and Fiona's former home, via Royston in Hertfordshire, but otherwise the action is centred on Marcus's and Will's flats and Marcus's school.
Highbury and Holloway (famous for its women's prison) are both located in the London Borough of Islington. Highbury is the site of the stadium of the famous Arsenal Football Club and also the home of author Nick Hornby himself. Islington consists to a great extent of housing built for the working and middle classes in the early to mid 19th century. Many of the larger houses have been converted into flats, and it is in one such flat that Marcus and his mother live. The population of the Borough, with an area of 15 square kilometres, is around 200,000 (a density of over 12,000 people per square kilometre) and its ethnic composition is 75% White, 12% Black (Afro-Caribbean) and 5.5% Asian, the remainder including 1.7% Chinese.
By contrast, the university city where Marcus and his parents used to live, Cambridge, has an area of 40 square kilometres with a population of around 111,000 (density 2,700 per square kilometre) and a racial composition of 90% White, 4% Asian, 1.3% Black (Afro-Caribbean) and 2% Chinese. It is thus easy to see that, in moving to London, Marcus will find himself in an entirely different ethnic and urban environment.
Little need be said about the small but historic town of Royston, situated about 20 kilometres south-west of Cambridge. The comment made in the book by Ruth, the owner of the music shop whose window is smashed by Ellie, that only the death of Julio Iglesias (not that of Kurt Cobain) could be exploited by a record-shop owner, tells us enough about the people who live here. Royston is a middle-class stronghold with agricultural links.

1.2 Time

The action of the novel takes place in the nine or ten months between the beginning of the school year in September 1993 and April or May 1994. The year is clearly mentioned in connection with the New Year's Eve parties that make up Chapters 23 and 24, and the closing chapters of the book are datable

by the historical fact of pop singer Kurt Cobain's suicide on April 8th 1994. Apart from these two dates, November 19th is specifically mentioned at the beginning of Chapter 18 as the first time in that year when the Christmas song "Santa's Super Sleigh" is played in public, marking an even earlier start to the Christmas season than the year before.
Compared to most novels of this length, the action covers a relatively brief period of intense emotional changes in the main characters. During this period Britain was governed by the Conservative party under prime minister John Major, who had replaced the "Iron Lady" Margaret Thatcher in 1990. A rather colourless politician, Major presided over a disastrous campaign which, under the slogan "Back to Basics", attempted to bring back the values of stable family life to a country where the traditional two-parent family unit was being replaced by emancipated feminist single-parenting. The "Back to Basics" campaign ran from 1994 to 1997, but revelations about John Major's four-year affair with a fellow Conservative politician Edwina Currie from 1984 to 1988 sabotaged both the campaign and John Major's chances of winning the 1997 elections.
So the book is set during a period when the facts of family life contradicted the ideals of a government which, despite the improving economic situation and slowly falling unemployment, seemed sometimes hopelessly out of touch with the mood of the nation.

2. Characters

2.1 Relationship diagrams

Brackets indicate relationships that have been ended. Square brackets indicate relationships invented by Will. The symbol † indicates people who have died.
Marcus's friends Mark and Nicky drop him in Chapter 5, so they are not listed here.

At the beginning of the novel

Will Freeman (an only child)		**Marcus Brewer** (an only child)		
Family:	Friends:	Family:	Family friends:	Own friends:
0	John & Christine	**Fiona**	Suzie	0
(mother) †	(Jessica)		SPAT	
(father) †	(various short-term girlfriends)	Clive →	Lindsey	
[ex-wife 'Paula']			Lindsey's mother	
[son 'Ned']				
(stepbrother/stepsister)				

Or, seen in terms of Marcus's "human pyramid" theory:

Will	**Marcus**	
+	+	
(a collection of 'fair-weather' friends)	Fiona (suicidal depressive)	Clive (separated 'ex-father')

At the end of the novel

Will Freeman (an only child) ←→ **Marcus Brewer** (an only child)

Family:	Friends:	Family:	Family friends:	Own friends:
0	John & Christine	→ **Fiona**	Suzie	**Ellie**
(mother) †	(Jessica)		SPAT	
(father) †	♥ → **Rachel**	Clive →	Lindsey	
	Ali ←		Lindsey's mother	

Or, seen in terms of Marcus's "human pyramid" theory:

Will			**Marcus**			
+			+			
Rachel	Marcus		Fiona	Will		
+			+			
Ali	Ellie	Fiona	Ali	Ellie	Clive	Lindsey etc.

2.2 Individual characters

2.2.1 Marcus

Marcus Brewer is a serious 12-year-old who wears glasses (always a disadvantage to children of his age), who sings to himself during classes and who, thanks mainly to his mother Fiona, is about the 'un-trendiest' boy at his new school.

At home he worries about his depressive mother and at school he is bullied by the other children. Even the headmistress can only advise him to "keep out of the way" of the bullies – not easy at a large comprehensive school in a rough neighbourhood. Life had been simpler at his school in Cambridge.

Even outside school his behaviour and clothing are unusual for a boy of his age. Will's first impression of him: "He had a strange frizzy bush of hair, and he dressed like a twenty-five-year-old chartered accountant on his day off: he was wearing brand-new jeans and a Microsoft T-shirt." (p. 49) He hates football, and when Will, who is "to all intents and purposes […] a teenager" himself, tries to "strike up a sparky, mutually curious relationship" with him in order to impress Suzie, the single mother whom he hopes to make his new girlfriend, by asking Marcus about his favourite sports and pop singers, Marcus asks – to Will's embarrassment – if he is getting the questions out of a book.

Despite the sympathy which the reader feels for Marcus, the boy shows several characteristics which Will recognizes as qualities of a "devious [= cunning, scheming] man" (p. 130): he stores up stupid things which his dad's girlfriend says or does as "ammunition" to tell his mother; he blackmails Will into allowing him to visit him and into "dating" Fiona; he "does deals" with Will on the level of an equal partner (when he agrees to pretend to be Will's son, for example); he quickly discovers the weak points of the adults around him ("What was it with this kid?" Will asks himself. "Once he had seen where you were *vulnerable*, he was merciless", p. 50; italics by P. N. H.); on Dead Duck Day the remarks he makes to Will and Suzie make them feel "old and beaten and found out" (p. 51).

Nor is Marcus always a passive victim: he disobeys his mother by going back regularly to Will's flat (p. 135); he loses his temper with his headmistress (p. 139) and with his parents (p. 264); he eats meat at the Christmas party just to shock his mother (p. 166); he plays truant after losing his temper with Mrs Morrison.

With his "human pyramid" theory, Marcus develops into a philosopher at the end of the book, so that even 36-year-old Will feels he is being "patronized" by a boy too young to understand the meaning of the word. "He [Will] was really struggling to maintain the age gap now: Marcus's air of authority, the been-there-done-that tone in his voice, was so convincing that Will didn't know how to argue with him." (p. 276)

So although Marcus definitely appears to be one of life's losers at the start of the novel, especially when the first time that he actually manages to *do* something he *wanted* to do (to hit a duck with a piece of bread) results in the death of the duck, he appears to be older, more mature than Will even, at the end of the book. His feelings of guilt at having killed the duck are removed by the strange vision which he has of his mother. He thinks he sees her in the park and turns round to point her out to Will and Suzie. But when he turns back, his mother is gone.

Dead Duck Day marks a turning point in Marcus's life, for this is the day when he returns from a picnic, walks into his flat "and a new part of his life began, bang, without any warning at all." (p. 57) His mother has tried to kill herself by taking an overdose of tablets. This experience turns him into "the oldest twelve-year-old in London", and he realizes that "two is not enough". If Fiona had died, he would have been alone. He spends a lot of time early in the novel trying to bring Will and Fiona together to provide the "back-up" which he needs. There is much humour in the description of this teenage matchmaking in Chapter 13, where Marcus tries to start up a conversation between Will and his mother.

Will realizes that what Marcus needs is not a father figure but "help to be a kid", so he buys him a pair of trendy, expensive Adidas trainers which are later stolen. Marcus's bad luck brings Will even deeper into commitment towards the Brewers. Then Marcus has a lucky break at school. Paradoxically, it is Marcus's very weirdness that makes two 15-year-old punk girls, Ellie and Zoe, "adopt" him. He says things that make them laugh (p. 151).

He develops a crush on Ellie, the fierce, rebellious punk, and finds that he can talk quite freely to his friend Will about it. Will himself uses Marcus as a confidant when he falls in love with Rachel, and Marcus willingly plays the part of Will's son in Chapters 26 and 27. Despite death threats from Rachel's son Ali, Marcus cheerfully – and perhaps embarrassingly for the adults – announces that Will "really fancies" Rachel. "He told me!" (p. 201)

Marcus does not mind being Ellie's "pet" as long as he can be with her. It is only later that he discovers that Ellie's rebellious nature is largely self-induced. She gets into trouble mainly because she wants to be and enjoys being a rebel. "Ellie spent her whole time wanting life to be shit" (p. 248) while his own life is "really shit for him, what with his mum and the other kids at school and all that, and he'd give anything to be Ellie […]. Ellie was like Will. If either of them had real trouble in their lives, they wouldn't want or need to invent it for themselves, or put pictures of it on the walls." (p. 249)

Marcus's character has developed greatly by the end of the book. He is really beginning to think for himself, just as his mother has always wanted him to. He realizes that it is too late for his father, Clive, to be a "proper dad". Marcus even tells him to his face: "I suppose you are a useless father, and that doesn't help a kid very much, but you'd have been a useless father wherever you were living" (p. 255).

He finally realizes that Ellie is not right for him, and that he needs a friend who is "less different". This leads the adults into a discussion about finding such a partner and causes Will to wonder whether he is happy with his own role as a "loner".

Marcus is thus a catalyst: he involves Will in his school problems first, then helps Will finally to understand – but not to solve – Fiona's problems. He willingly plays the part of Will's son in order to make him appear more interesting to Rachel and generally involves Will in the lives of other people, thus assisting Will's development from "one of life's visitors" into a real, caring human being.

At the end of the book, Marcus has played a great part in solving his own problems. He loses himself (in the sense that he is no longer the weird, bullied outsider at school) and has the friends that he needed so badly at the beginning of the novel.

2.2.2 Will

"Being men's-magazine cool was as close as he had ever come to an achievement" (p. 6) is almost the first thing we learn about Will Freeman. This is a devastating criticism. Will has no family, no job – no life even. "You didn't need to have a life of your own any more," is what he tells himself, "you could just peek over the fence at other people's lives" (p. 6).

Perhaps he really believes this, but as we find out more about him we discover that he has problems coping with his empty life. He is proud of the way he has divided the time when other people are normally at work into half-hour units, but this ingenuity is itself a product of having nothing much to do. As Rachel realizes late in the book (p. 226), "There's nothing between you and despair, and you don't seem a very desperate person."

That is because Will has organized his life so well that (if we are to believe him) "he wondered how his friends could juggle life and a job. Life took up so much time, so how could one work *and*, say, take a bath on the same day?" (p. 72) This is a comic exaggeration, of course: most of the time Will is very busy doing nothing – or next to nothing – and is well aware of this fact, even though he dare not admit it to himself.

"He may have been good-looking and articulate, but that was just a quirk of genetics, environment and education; at his core he was ugly and monosyllabic" is Will's pessimistic summary of himself when he first meets Rachel (p. 172). He is a loner. He is selfish. Even his protestation, when Fiona calls him a "selfish bastard", that he is on his own: "There's just me. I'm not putting myself first, because there isn't anybody else" (p. 133) only emphasizes his selfishness. And also, sadly, his loneliness.

He goes shopping for clothes and CDs. He drives aimlessly around London listening to loud music that would otherwise have driven his neighbours crazy. He has even applied for jobs and tried to do voluntary social work, but these things have always been done "in the same spirit that he had become the father of Ned; it was all a dreamy alternative reality that didn't touch his real life, whatever that was, at all." (p. 72) Note the hint of self-criticism in the ironic phrase "whatever that was", for Will increasingly realizes that you cannot just be a visitor to life (he still calls himself "one of life's visitors" as late as p. 93). His apparently full and well-organized day is simply a defence mechanism to stay on the surface of life (surface and superficial are, after all, cognate words) and to avoid being dragged under the water by boredom and a sense of his own uselessness.

Until he meets Marcus, he has avoided any kind of deep involvement in other people's problems. "No problem was his problem. Very few people were in a position to say they had no problems, but then that wasn't his problem either." (p. 106) Nevertheless, he soon sees that he is "serving some purpose in the kid's life" (p. 103).

The phrase "No problem was his problem" can be given a deeper significance: having no problems is actually Will's real problem. He lacks commitment and involvement. If he had to solve problems of his own, he would soon become involved in other people's problems because they would probably be the *cause* of his many of his problems.

At last Will, at the age of 36, slowly begins a search for a "life of his own" while still keeping his cynical view that "loving people, and allowing yourself to be loved, was only worth the risk if the odds were in your favour" (p. 131). Until he falls in love with Rachel, the risk still seems too high. At their first meeting he searches desperately for some aspect of his jobless life that might make him interesting to her and accidentally 'invents' yet another son: Marcus.

Will knows that love – and involvement in other people's lives – will make him unhappy. Even when Fiona insists that he cannot just shut life out, he still feels that she is wrong: "She was wrong, he was almost positive. You could shut life out. If you didn't answer the door to it, how was it going to get in?" (p. 133) By page 243, however, Will has been forced to realize that *everybody's* problem is his problem – and that he has no solutions to any of them.

By the time he is driving Fiona's and Ellie's mother Katrina to Royston to pick up Marcus and Ellie from the police station, he is forced to admit to himself that "Life was, after all, like air. [...] There seemed to be no way of keeping it out [...] and all he could do for the moment was live it and breathe it. How people managed to draw it down into their lungs without choking was a mystery to him; it was full of bits. This was air you could almost chew." (p. 256)

At Royston police station, caught up in the messy, chaotic web of human relationships which he has successfully avoided for so long, Will gets "a glimpse of what it was like to be human. It wasn't too bad, really; he wouldn't even mind being human on a full-time basis" (pp. 264–265). When Fiona and Katrina agree that they are single because they spend half their lives looking for someone "less different" from themselves, Will wonders if this applies to his own life. Because Rachel is *not* like Will: she is "dynamic and thoughtful and focused and caring" (p. 266). Katrina's logic only works if a person *thinks* he or she is not so bad in the first place.

So perhaps if Will becomes more like Rachel and less like the old selfish Will, they will come closer together. At the end of the book, Will has "lost his shell and his cool and his distance, and he felt scared and vulnerable, but he got to be with Rachel" (p. 278), which is now what he wants most out of his new life.

One aspect of Will's character which should be mentioned is his fear of embarrassment. This peculiarly British phobia, not always apparent to foreigners, accounts for the proverbial coolness, politeness and reserved nature of the English character. This politeness is the result of not wishing to embarrass others or to be embarrassed by them in turn. If a foreigner asks an English person to say exactly what he or she thinks, the response is usually less – and often far less – than the truth. Because saying what one thinks might hurt or offend the other person. Will gives a good example of this when he asks Marcus to pretend to be his son because Rachel has convinced herself that he is. He tries to explain to Marcus that he does not want to embarrass her. To the English temperament, politeness always has precedence over correctness (even truth). Will recalls the neighbour who has always called him Bill and probably always would because Will had not told him right from the start that his name was not Bill (p. 187). Like most English people, Will would do almost anything to avoid embarrassment, and the novel is full of scenes where embarrassment, or the wish to avoid it, play an important role.

2.2.3 Fiona

"[...] it seemed to Will that Fiona was a peculiarly contemporary creation, with her seventies albums, her eighties politics and her nineties foot lotion" (p. 111). A humorous description of a 38-year-old hippy living in a world of grunge music and rap!

Fiona is a music therapist earning £400 a week. Not a lot of money even in those days. She is a vegetarian and has kept many of her hippy traditions alive (music, clothing, hairstyle, ideals). She has even been to India, the Mecca of the hippy generation. But she suffers from depression. She and her boyfriend Roger split up in Chapter 1, in Chapter 5 she is already crying at the breakfast table and in Chapter 9 she tries to commit suicide.

Although she tells her son that she wants him to think for himself, she spends a lot of time forcing him to accept her own views on life. She cuts Marcus's hair herself (the other kids at school call him "Fuzzy", so these haircuts are not a great success) and makes sure he wears "sensible" (i.e. non-trendy) clothes. While Marcus himself admits that he is a "weird kid", his mother's strict ideas and her insistence that he should be an "individual" make him even weirder. There is more than a hint of the feminist idea that children do not really need a father in Fiona's character. She resents Will's influence over Marcus at first and tries to stop Marcus from seeing him. When, during one of their "arguments", she forces Marcus to give her a good reason for seeing Will, Marcus says: "Because I need a father." (p. 122) He says this mainly in order to win the argument, not because he really means it. But this has always been Fiona's greatest fear. "I was very upset," she tells Will later. "I felt as though I'd been slapped round the face." (p. 129)

Fiona is full of **commitment**. She worries about Marcus's "emotional honesty" (p. 131) and in many other ways belongs to a different world than Will's. Will's friendship with Marcus involves him more and more in her problems. It is only when she tells him that she needs sympathy and understanding, not solutions from "a bloke in Essex Road who can fix it" that Will realizes he can help her by just listening to her problems not by wanting, as men traditionally do, to try and "fix" things.

In a highly comic scene at Royston police station, Fiona makes a fool of herself by overdoing her protective mother role. "[...] she had decided that the time for action was now. [...] once she had decided to fight for her child she was unstoppable" (p. 263). She appeals over-dramatically to the policewoman "as a mother" to give her and Marcus "another chance" despite Marcus's protests that he has done nothing wrong.

At the end of the book, Fiona has "lost a big chunk of Marcus, and she got to stay away from the casualty ward" (p. 278). She is no longer likely to "top herself" (= commit suicide), which was Marcus's greatest fear.

2.2.4 Ellie

Eleanor Toyah Gray is 15. She has a reputation for always being in trouble at school. Like Marcus and Rachel's son Ali, she is being brought up by a single mother, Katrina.

Ellie and her friend Zoe "adopt" Marcus as a kind of mascot because he is cute and makes them laugh with his weird, serious attitudes and statements. Her friendship is an important turning point in Marcus's problematic school life, and he even tells Will that he does not mind being a kind of pet. Ellie is also the first person of around Marcus's age with whom he can have a serious talk about his problems at the New Year's Eve party in Chapter 25.

Ellie says exactly what she thinks. She calls her own mother a "SAD OLD TART" when she and Marcus catch Katrina kissing a man outside in the garden at the party (p. 185), but Ellie is a rebel on principle. She uses the usual rebellious clichés. When Marcus asks her why she thinks that "life is shit", she replies: "Because ... because the world is sexist and racist and full of injustice." (p. 249) Marcus knows this is true, but he realizes that Ellie spends her whole time wanting life to be shit. "You have too good a time," Marcus tells her on the same page.
Ellie's gesture of rebellion against the exploitation of the suicide of her pop idol Kurt Cobain – smashing the window of a record shop in Royston – is shown in a comic light when the record-shop owner turns out to be a woman who is dressed like and actually looks like Ellie's older sister, and who turns out to be a great Cobain fan, too.
In a way, Ellie can be considered a gentle parody of youthful feminist rebellion. But she plays an important role in protecting Marcus at school and in developing his character.

2.2.5 Rachel

Rachel is the most stable character in the novel. Although she is a single mother, we get the impression that she has her situation under complete control. She is "an intelligent, cultured, ambitious, beautiful, witty and single woman" (p. 171), and thinking about her gives Will "a glimpse of what life could be like if he were in any way interesting" (p. 172).
At the New Year's Eve party where he meets Rachel, Will desperately searches for something interesting to talk to her about. He misses Ned, the imaginary son intended to make him interesting to single mothers at the single parents' group SPAT, which Will joins early in the novel. Even when Rachel asks about Will's connection with Robert, who is giving the party, he can only reply, rather pathetically: "I used to buy my dope [= drugs] off him years ago" – before Robert had become a successful television producer.
The situation is saved when, talking about the musical tastes of twelve-year-olds, Rachel imagines that Will has a son the same age as her son Ali. So indirectly she forces Will to realize that "the most interesting thing about his life [...] was Marcus" (p. 174).
Will has not actually lied to Rachel, but when he decides to explain who Marcus actually is, he becomes involved in a hilarious dialogue (pp. 206–209) where he even tries to blame Rachel for assuming that Marcus was his son! Luckily, Rachel is honest, tolerant and has a sense of humour. As Will stumbles on through his explanations of half-lies, Rachel shows "a quiet amusement and a sort of baffled tolerance", small mercies for which Will is endlessly grateful. But it is obvious that there is a long way to go before their friendship can develop beyond the stage of "a quick hair-ruffle" (p. 209).

Rachel is honest with Will: "I thought you were a sort of blank – you didn't do anything, you weren't passionate about anything, you didn't have much to say – and then when you said you had a kid –" Rachel wants to make Will feel better when she says: "You didn't make it all up about Marcus. You're involved, and you care, and you understand him, and you worry about him … So you're not the guy I thought you were before you brought him up." (p. 210)
It is Rachel who points out to Will that Marcus "adores" him (p. 224), something which Will had not thought about before. What Rachel tells Will convinces him that he has wasted thirty-six years. He knows now, at last, that he "wanted his own life, and his own identity; he wanted to be interesting in his own right. […] He had somehow turned himself into a single parent without even going to the trouble of fathering a child." (p. 210) The reason why some of the parents at SPAT have problems, Will sees now, is not because they have children but because they fell in love and made themselves **vulnerable**. Will has fallen in love with Rachel and is in the same position. He "deserved all he got. He'd be singing with his eyes closed soon, and there was nothing he could do about it." (p. 211)
It is Rachel who, when talking about "the point of life", points out to a confused Will: "You don't need a point … you have to be fairly tough in your head to do what you do" (i.e. to do *nothing*, p. 225). "Because … most of us think that the point is something to do with work, or kids, or family, or whatever. But you don't have any of that. There's nothing between you and despair, and you don't seem a very desperate person. […] The point is you keep going. You want to. So all the things that make you want to are the point." (p. 226)
Rachel is an optimist, and her "simple positivity" is followed almost immediately by an invitation to her bed. This is Will's first sexual encounter with the woman he loves.

2.2.6 Clive

Perhaps the saddest figure at the end of the novel is Clive. As he and Fiona were never married, we do not even know his surname. He is a shadowy character until the end of the book, where he is highlighted to illustrate an important "male problem": the "failed ex-father". Even when parents have split up, it must be sad to be a separated father whose 12-year-old son feels sorry for him.
Marcus "couldn't really see what his dad could offer him any more, which was why he was sorry for him" (p. 267). Marcus has no real respect for his father. At Royston police station, Marcus loses his temper and shouts: "Bloody hell, I can't believe how crap my parents are."
When Clive tries to adopt the role of the authoritarian parent on the drive back to Cambridge, Marcus just lets him moan on until he seems "to run out

of moans like you run out of petrol [...]. The thing was, he couldn't be that kind of dad [= a respected parent entitled to 'moan' about his child's behaviour] any more. He'd missed his moment." (p. 267)
Clive has some sort of job with Cambridge Social Services (Marcus is not sure what he does, but knows that he "doesn't earn much", p. 105). During Marcus's weekend visits to Cambridge, Clive does not seem to do much with his son. Marcus watches a lot of TV and on Sundays they visit Clive's girlfriend's mother who lives on the Norfolk coast.
Even Clive's modest victories over caffeine and nicotine addiction seem only to be mentioned by Marcus in one of his comic conversations with Will (pp. 104–106) because Marcus's own life is so triumph-free at that moment. Although Clive may not smoke cigarettes, he does, however, smoke joints.
Even falling off a window-ledge and breaking his collar bone while doing some simple DIY job is treated as a piece of light comedy by the author. Marcus repeats the phrase "when you fell off the window ledge" several times during their "serious" father-to-son talk on pages 269–271 because it "sounded so daft". His "accident", as Clive prefers to call it, hardly puts him in the dramatic category of the man in one of the newspaper articles on Marcus's bedroom wall: "MAN FALLS FIVE THOUSAND FEET AND LIVES [...]. Those were the sort of things that made you have a big think about your life, not falling off a window-ledge while you were pretending to be a proper dad." (p. 231)
Clive's "big think about life" is thus treated as something slightly comical right from the start ("He fell off a window-ledge. No wonder his [Marcus's] mum had cheered up", p. 230), and this comedy is mirrored in the humorous contrast between Clive's hippy-like appearance and his pompous protests to Katrina at Royston police station about Ellie's behaviour, which "didn't really suit a man wearing a University of Life sweatshirt and a plaster cast" (p. 261).
Even the results of Clive's "big think" are not so big. He thinks that it was wrong of him to leave Fiona because he believes that Marcus needs a father. But Marcus knows that his dad "couldn't have it both ways. If he wanted to be up in Cambridge with Lindsey, smoking pot and falling off window-ledges, fine, but he couldn't then start picking up on the little things [...]. He'd have to find another job for himself. Will could do the little things, and his mum, but his dad was out of it." (p. 268) Marcus explains his "human pyramid" theory and tells Clive that he knows where to find him if he needs him.
If Hornby intends us to believe that all separated fathers are like Clive, all the reader can say is: "Ex-dads? Forget them!" But Hornby's own deep commitment to his autistic son Daniel shows that the author has his own very positive views on fatherhood despite the fact that he is now divorced.

3. Point of View

The author of a novel or short story has a choice of various ways of telling that story. If he or she wishes the reader to 'see' the action through the eyes of the main or one of the main protagonists, the **first-person narration** is normally chosen. The reader is thus given one person's point of view, and words like "I", "me", "my", "mine", "we", "us", "our" etc. feature frequently in the narrative. When such a first-person narrator 'tells' the reader about the actions of other people which he or she observes, however, the reader is limited to the narrator's point of view unless the other people speak for themselves by using direct speech. However, the protagonist's interpretation of and reaction to such second-person dialogues is again restricted to his or her point of view.

By definition, first-person narration is **subjective**. The reader also assumes a much closer relationship between the author and the narrator. Often they are, or wish to be, the same person. Authors using this style of narration certainly identify – and thus sympathize – much more with their main protagonists.

Third-person narration, also by definition, is **objective**. The author is outside the action. The narrative text puts equal stress on characters who are just "he", "she" or "they". The pronouns "I" and "we" only occur in dialogue. If they occur in statements made in the narrative text, we can be sure that such statements are intended as **author's comments** addressed directly to the reader.

The author of a third-person narrative has a **global point of view**. Like God, he or she "sees all, knows all and tells all". He or she is up in the air, so to speak, looking down, on the action, telling the reader what is happening or what the characters are thinking, whereas the author of a first-person narrative is basically telling the story **subjectively** from inside his or her first-person narrator, who is often trying hard to understand what is going on from his or her limited viewpoint.

A third-person narrative can be written from the point of view of **one third-person** who is present throughout the book or from the point of view of **two or more persons** who appear in different parts of the book, often in completely different contexts which may or may not be brought together as the action develops. In either case, the author tells the story from a distance and does not associate closely with the main protagonist(s), though he or she may comment on the protagonist's thoughts or feelings. An extension of this form of narration is the even more objective **camera-eye view** where the author stays outside the thoughts and feelings of the protagonist(s), presenting the story as an objective eyewitness.

About a Boy falls into the category of a third-person narrative seen exclusively through the eyes of two persons: Marcus and Will. Notice that both the main protagonists are male, underlying Nick Hornby's preoccupation with male problems. Despite this preoccupation, Hornby skilfully stands apart from the problems he is describing, allowing the reader to make his or her own conclusions. He avoids the moralizing tone, using humour to emphasize his points. Instead of stones, the school bullies throw *hard sweets* at Marcus when they follow him to Will's flat. The brutal gesture of bullying remains the same, but it is softened slightly by the choice of projectile.

Both first-person and third-person narratives involve dialogues, which we may call **second-person narrative** (implying the "you" person of conversation – all stage plays, films and operas are second-person narratives) and here the author is uninvolved, presenting to the reader what his or her characters say to each other directly. The main difference here is that in a first-person narrative, the narrator is often involved in dialogue, whereas the narrator in a third-person narrative is the **author**, who hardly ever 'steps into' dialogues to discuss things with a character (the appearance of Paul Auster in *City of Glass* is a rare example) and who may be quite a different person from the 'real' author.

About a Boy is a third-person narrative which starts with two story lines (see "Form and Structure", p. 71) and two quite separate main protagonists, Marcus Brewer and Will Freeman.

The narrative proceeds in a literally straightforward chronological sequence, in the present, with no big jumps backwards or forwards in time except in cases where the two story lines, continued in consecutive chapters, involve taking up the story line from the point where it left off at the end of the preceding chapter. But this is hardly genuine flashback technique. A good example of the dramatic use of mentioning something which has already happened *before* the chapter describing it is when Fiona and Will hear of Marcus and Ellie's arrest by the police at the end of Chapter 32 before the events actually leading up to it are narrated in Chapter 33.

The technique of introducing genuine **flashbacks** into the past is limited to past events which are responsible for a character's behaviour in the present. Pages 7–9 take the reader back one week only into the past, when Will visits his friends John and Christine. It is the longest flashback in the book. All other flashbacks are short. Will's memories of past girlfriends (especially Jessica) are used by Will to justify his no-commitment existence. An early "flashback within a flashback" even appears in brackets to mark it as such:

> "(He still saw her [Jessica], sometimes, for a lunchtime pizza, and she would show him pictures of her children, and tell him he was wasting his life, and he didn't know what it was like, and she would tell him he couldn't handle it anyway, and he would tell her he had no intention of finding out one way or the other; then they would sit in silence and glare at each other.) (p. 9)

4. Mode of Presentation

As this novel is mainly concerned with the development of human relationships and personalities, there is hardly any **scenic description**. We are given no detailed descriptions of the layout of Marcus's or Will's flats. There is no description of the area of North London where they live. We are given names of actual streets in the area (Upper Street, Essex Road) but no details about them. The only reference to Islington's multicultural and problematic racial mix comes on p. 39 when Marcus goes into a newsagent's shop run by Mr and Mrs Patel. We are told that the Patels are friendly with his mother because she talks to them "about the place where they came from; she had been there once, a long time ago, when she was a real hippy." Some boys, who have followed Marcus into the shop and put sweets in his pockets to make it look as if he was stealing, shout: "Oi, Mohammed! [...] You ought to check his pockets. He's been thieving!" As Patel is a typical Indian surname, it is more likely that the Patels are Hindus, not Moslems.

About a Boy is not concerned with places or social problems like racism. So the narrative concentrates on describing the thoughts of the main characters. There are long passages of **internal monologue** where Marcus's and Will's thoughts are presented to the reader. Often these thoughts supplement dialogue, but frequently they contrast the differences between what the character is really thinking and what he (for the only two characters whose thoughts we are given are both male) is actually saying.

This **contrast of inner thoughts and actual situation** is often used to make the reader laugh, as when Will's friend Christine shows him her week-old baby daughter Imogen and Will is at a loss for words (p.7), which shows his naive attitude towards parenting.

Sometimes this kind of contrast is **cynical**. During the scene where Angie takes all responsibility for ending her short relationship with Will because of her own problems with her ex-husband Simon, Will's apparently aggressive verbal reaction is followed by a cynical internal comment on his real mental reaction expressing his own subliminal contempt for himself:

> "'Is he giving you a hard time? Because if he is ...' You'll what? he wanted to ask himself contemptuously. You'll roll yourself a joint when you get home and forget them? You'll go out with someone a lot easier?" (p. 23)

Sometimes the contrast produces **irony**, as when Angie, further down the same page, shows how little – luckily for Will – she understands Will's motives in making her his girlfriend when she says: "The tragedy is that I've met someone just right for me at precisely the wrong time. I should have started with a meaningless fling" (p. 23). The irony lies in Will's realization that, for him, his relationship with Angie has been exactly that: a "meaningless fling".

He is exactly the right person for a meaningless sexual fling. But it is too late to save the relationship by confessing that he is much shallower than Angie realizes.

As inner monologue is restricted to Will and Marcus, the author lets his other protagonists reveal their characters through **dialogue**. Fiona's confused state of mind is revealed in what Will calls her "logic-free lectures" (p. 159) in the course of which she involves herself in much self-contradiction as, for instance, when she phones Will after Marcus has told her that he needs a father figure. She begins by stating the opposite: "Marcus doesn't need a father, and he certainly doesn't need a father like you." Then she puts Marcus's own opinion: "Marcus seems to think he needs adult male company. A father figure. And somehow your name came up." Finally she gives up because she cannot make herself clear and does not get through to Will who, in her view, seems to "resort to sarcasm" (pp. 126–127).

Fiona does not like **sarcasm**, though the only slightly sarcastic comment in this context is the justifiable reference to the fact that Cambridge is barely 90 kilometres from North London. Sarcasm, of course, is a type of humour provoked by another person's failure to appreciate the realities (or simplicity) of a situation. No wonder Will is "beginning to feel as though this telephone conversation was going to be his life's work; that once every few hours he would put the receiver down to eat and sleep and go to the toilet, and the rest of the time Fiona would be telling him one thing and then its opposite over and over again." (p. 127)

Sarcasm, often defined as "the lowest form of wit", is used frequently, often in order to stress a problematic response to what the speaker thinks is a simple situation. Marcus normally has no sense of sarcasm. When Will suggests that Marcus should try to disguise his weirdness from other kids to avoid being bullied, Marcus takes his suggestion quite literally:

> "'What, with a moustache and stuff?
> 'Yeah, right, with a moustache. Nobody would notice a twelve-year-old boy with a moustache, would they?'
> Marcus looked at him. 'You're joking. Everyone would notice. I'd be the only one in the whole school.'
> Will had forgotten about the sarcasm thing." (p. 110)

Mostly, the author develops the plot through the actions, thoughts and dialogues of the main protagonists, but very occasionally he speaks directly to the reader. This happens twice in Chapter 2, when we meet Will for the first time:

> "The twenty-year-old Will would have been surprised and perhaps disappointed to learn that he would reach the age of thirty-six without finding a life for himself." (p. 7)

and:

> "A couple of weeks later Will met Angie and became a temporary stepfather for the first time. Maybe if he had swallowed his pride and his hatred of children and the family and domesticity and monogamy and early nights, he could have saved himself an awful lot of trouble." (p. 10)

Otherwise, the author stands well back from the action of his novel, allowing dialogue and the protagonists' thoughts to drive the action forward.

5. Form and Structure

About a Boy is structured around two story lines which are presented separately at first and then, when the protagonists meet and the story lines combine, in alternate chapters where the action is seen through the eyes of either Marcus or Will. Presenting the two story lines separately at the beginning of the novel (Marcus in Chapters 1, 3, 5 and 7, Will in Chapters 2, 4 and 6) generates curiosity: the reader cannot wait to find out what could possibly bring these two very different individuals together.

Story line 1 introduces 12-year-old Marcus Brewer, who is shown as a loser: his parents broke up four years before the story starts; he and his mother have just moved to London; his underpaid mother (aged 38) is best described as an ageing hippy with alternative and feminist views (later on she reveals herself as a suicidal depressive); Marcus is being bullied at his new school (a fact for which his mother's lifestyle is mainly responsible: he wears thick glasses, uncool clothes and is also in other respects "weird").

Story line 2 introduces 36-year-old Will Freeman, who is shown as a **winner**: he is cool, trendy, wealthy and does not have to work for a living; he is independent – he has no family ties but is handsome and has no trouble finding a new girlfriend when the previous one leaves him. Will is introduced in Chapter 2, and the reader is given the impression, even by Will himself (who says "I really am this shallow", p. 9), that he is perhaps disappointed with his comfortable but superficial lifestyle, though he dare not admit it to himself.

The story-lines merge in Chapter 8, but the chapter scenarios continue to alternate between Marcus's and Will's viewpoints until the end of the book, and although the main protagonists, of course, share many of the chapters, it is the **viewpoint of the main protagonist** in each chapter that gives the reader insight into what is going on (see Table p. 72).

Ch.	Appearance of Protagonists and Viewpoints (= X) of each Chapter			What happens:
	Who appears in which chapter?			
	Marcus	**Both**	**Will**	
	Through whose eyes is the action seen?			
1	X			Introducing Marcus
2			X	Introducing Will
3	X			Marcus's school problems; losing his only friends
4			X	Will and Angie
5	X			Fiona's depression; Marcus at school
6			X	Will joins SPAT and invents Ned
7	X			Fiona's depression gets worse
8		Will		Dead Duck Day
9		Marcus		Fiona's attempted suicide
10		Will		Fiona is taken to hospital
11	X			Fiona comes home
12		Will		Marcus phones Will
13		Marcus		Fiona and Will's first date
14		Will		Marcus's first visit to Will
15		Marcus		More visits to Will's flat
16		Will		Will buys Marcus some trainers
17		Marcus		Fiona confronts Will
18		Will		Will's discussion with Fiona
19	X			Marcus meets Ellie and plays truant
20		Will		Will tells Marcus about Kurt Cobain
21	X			Ellie and Zoe "adopt" Marcus
22		Will		Christmas: Will's view
23		Marcus		Christmas: Marcus's view
24			X	Will falls in love
25	X			Marcus's New Year's Eve
26		Will		Marcus becomes Will's son
27		Marcus		Lunch with Rachel and Ali
28			X	Will confesses to Rachel
29		Marcus		Fiona goes into depression again
30			X	Will goes to bed with Rachel
31	X			Marcus and Ellie go to Cambridge
32			X	More discussion with Fiona
33	X			In trouble with the police
34		Will		At the police station in Royston
35	X			Marcus talks to his father
36		Will		All's well that ends well

So although both protagonists appear in many of the chapters, we see each chapter only through the eyes of one of them. The viewpoint of the third-person narrator alternates from Marcus to Will throughout the whole book whether or not they both appear in the chapter. There is a perfect balance of points of view (starting with Marcus in Chapter 1 and ending with Will in Chapter 36): both protagonists view the action alternately in eighteen of the thirty-six chapters.
There are also exactly eighteen chapters which feature both main protagonists. Of the other eighteen chapters, Marcus has the lion's share with eleven to himself while Will only has seven, but it would be a mistake, perhaps, to pursue this 'numbers game' any further than saying that the novel is structurally nicely balanced in respect of viewpoint.

The **language** used in the dialogues of the novel is everyday standard middle-class British English. There is very occasional comic pomposity. Fiona's use of the verb "reiterate" on p. 130, or the mention of Will's "munificence" on p. 112, for instance: these are words which would send many native speakers of average intelligence running to their dictionaries.
There is much use of 'normal everyday' vulgarisms. The word "fucking" is used frequently but, as Marcus himself says: "It's OK. People say it at school all the time." (p. 102) Ironically, Will's normally banal statement "Fucking hell" (p. 102) has a deep significance for Marcus, as it shows his worrying about his mother's attempted suicide and its possible repetition is serious, not 'pathetic'. Less 'shocking' swear-words like "sod" ("Will wouldn't let the little sod [= Marcus] drag him under", p. 131), "sodding" ("Everything came back to the sodding baby", p. 7) are used less frequently. The words "shit" and "crap" are often used in the sense of 'terrible'. One example of the use of "shit", more humorous than it is vulgar, is when Marcus translates the French expression "*Tant pis*" used by Fiona on p. 42 as "tough shit". A more usual translation would be 'too bad'. Perhaps Marcus associated the French word "pis" with the English word "piss", hence the connection with "shit". The average English reader certainly would!
The abbreviation SPAT for the "Single Parents Alone Together" organization is not only the past tense of the verb 'to spit' but also a noun signifying a (slight) quarrel or argument between people. The author has, one feels, deliberately chosen this abbreviation not only for its comic effect but also for its tragic undertone: the contradiction of "alone together" is obvious. Will's thoughts on the organization as he observes the still-friendly relationship between Fiona and her ex-partner Clive at the Christmas party deserve mention in this context:

> "This couldn't happen all the time, Will thought, otherwise SPAT would have been full of happy but estranged couples all introducing their exes and their nexts and their kids from here, there and everywhere; but [...] it had been full of justified and righteous anger, and a very great deal of unhappiness." (p. 159)

The word "squillion" in the phrase "There were about seventy-nine squillion people in the world, and if you were lucky, you would end up being loved by fifteen or twenty of them" (p. 131) is an invention of the author. It is an example of the humorous use of **hyperbole** (perhaps pseudo-hyperbole, as the word "squillion" is itself an invention) emphasizing, despite the humorous touch, Will's bitter cynicism and pessimism in connection with lasting relationships.

There is some significance in the **choice of names** for the characters in the novel. Marcus is perhaps one of the least trendy names a boy could be given in the late 20th century. Ellie and Zoe even make a joke about it when they ask him his name:

> "'Marcus. Cool name.'
> 'Do you think so?' Marcus hadn't thought about his name that much, but he'd never thought it was cool.
> 'No,' said Ellie's friend, and they laughed again." (p. 149)

Marcus's father Clive also has an unusually untrendy first name, whereas Ellie's second name, Toyah, was chosen by her mother because she wanted her daughter to grow up like the feisty and rebellious English pop singer and actress Toyah Wilcox (p. 258).
William (short form: Will) can hardly be described as a trendy first name even for someone born in the 1950s. It is very middle-class. Perhaps there is a subconscious connection between Will's father's name (Charles) and Prince Charles (Prince William's father). There is nothing in Will's character to suggest that Hornby chose this name for any special reason. Certainly not because of any strength of will or will-power in his wimpish protagonist. But perhaps the author chose the surname Freeman for Will because Will thinks he is a free man.
The use of the short form Ali (for Rachel's son Alistair) at first suggests some connection with the Moslem community and would have been avoided twenty years ago. Nowadays, perhaps, its use implies that the old racial prejudices are rapidly being swept away in multicultural Britain.

6. Themes and Motifs

6.1 "Two is not enough" versus "Every man is an island"

The phrase "two is not enough" could almost be called the theme-song of the book. It occurs frequently throughout the novel. Marcus's idea of society based on the "human pyramid" (pp. 275–276) is obviously at least a part solution to the problem of the dysfunctional single-parent family. It is messier, perhaps, but certainly preferable to Will's selfish "every man is an island" philosophy.

This theme appears early in the film version of the novel in the form of the quotation from the poet John Donne (see p. 89): "No man is an island", an opinion which Will, in the film, rejects as "a load of bollocks [= rubbish]".

Marcus spends much of the book searching for the "back-up" which a two-member family obviously needs if the single mother is depressive and the son only twelve years old.

Will, who is dependent on nobody, soon discovers that he needs other people to give his life a point. He is forced to invent a two-year-old son and ex-wife in order to join SPAT, and later adopts Marcus in order to make himself more interesting to Rachel.

6.2 The family unit

Both Will and Marcus are only children. Will is the only child of his father's second marriage and has lost touch with his stepbrother and stepsister "who were old and dull anyway" (p. 124). We have the impression that Will's childhood was, in different ways, just as sad as Marcus's, despite the fact that there was plenty of money and security in Will's home. His family had been intact but just as dysfunctional as Marcus's; "but you didn't need dosh [= money] to be dysfunctional" (p. 126) is clearly a criticism of his own family circumstances.

The jolly Christmas song "Santa's Super Sleigh", the song which not only ruined his father's life (p. 124) but which Will's mother made him sing in front of various relations each Christmas (mainly, Will thinks, to punish her husband), has not only brought in a lot of money but also caused much unhappiness.

So it is not surprising that Will, whose own family life was apparently so unhappy, has no ambition to start a family of his own. He had his chance with his last long-term girlfriend Jessica, who abandoned him in order to find someone who would share the commitment of children and a family.

The only intact family unit described in the whole book is summarized by Will in one word: "Clutter!" (p. 7) His solitary life means that he can avoid clutter like this. He is "sure that they [John and Christine] were unhappy

even if they had achieved some peculiar, brain-washed state that prevented them from recognizing their own unhappiness." (p. 8)
We must not forget we are seeing family life through Will's cynical eyes, but we are given a clear picture of a cold, selfish egoist who thinks only of himself and wants no further contact with fans of the intact family unit: "He wouldn't be bothering with them again." (p. 9)
The other family units described in the book are more or less dysfunctional. The dysfunctional family unit, based on the modern idea of "single parenthood", is one of the great problems of British society in and around the turn of the millennium. *About a Boy* shows us several such units.

6.3 Single parenthood

This is an important theme. It is the background to the entire novel.
All parents in the book apart from the married couple John and Christine and Marcus's absent father Clive are **single mothers** (Angie and her two children; Suzie and Megan; Fiona and Marcus; Rachel and Ali; Katrina and Ellie). Brief mention is made of two **single fathers** (Jeremy at SPAT, whose wife was killed in a car crash, p. 36, and Stephen Wood's father who is introduced on p. 182 simply to enable Marcus to win an argument with Ellie, which he rarely does when talking to his mother) but it is obvious that there are very few of these. No matter what feminist arguments are brought forward, single mothers are seen in this novel as **vulnerable**. Will decides to exploit the position of a beautiful single woman (Angie) "who'd been messed around and eventually abandoned by the father of her children, and who hadn't met anyone since (because the kids stopped you going out and anyway a lot of men didn't like kids that didn't belong to them) … if you picked one of these, then she loved you for it. All of a sudden you became better-looking, a better lover, a better person. […] Sure, there were right-on [= moral, honest] people, men and women, who would be repelled and appalled by this logic, but that was fine by him. It reduced the competition." (p. 21) This is, of course, a very cynical point of view that would raise howls of protest at SPAT, but Will shamelessly decides to use the single-mothers' complaint that "all men are bastards" (p. 20) as an invitation to "clean up" [= to take whatever he wants]. "He decided that […] children served as a symbolic blemish, like a birthmark … which gave him a chance where previously there would have been none. Maybe children *democratized* beautiful single women." (p. 20)
Despite the humorously positive overtones of the word "democratize", few feminists would agree with these cynical views of a single male. Single motherhood should not be an invitation to marauders like Will, whose callous intentions reduce him from the role of a "wolf" to that of a hyena. Will is certainly punished for this selfish attitude in the later stages of the novel, but many female readers may feel that he is not punished enough.

What is missing in the broken relationship of a single-parent family is the kind of **commitment** (see p. 79), particularly **male commitment**, which Will spends most of the book trying to avoid – until he falls in love.
Will discovers early in the story that the single mothers at the SPAT party are the victims of : "Men who took one look at their new child and went, men who took one look at their new colleague and went, men who went for the hell of it [i.e. for no particular reason]. [...] by the time Suzie had finished her litany of treachery and deceit, he wanted to cut off his own penis with a kitchen knife" (p. 36) on the same impulse that the (presumably) pre-pubescent Marcus tells his mother that he wants a vasectomy: "He knew for a fact that he was never going to have children, so why not get it over and done with now?" (p. 43)
The humorous tone of the above quotations does not mean that the author is treating the subject lightly. It is one of the great qualities of this novel that it manages to describe serious issues in a humorous way.

6.4 Growing up

Although the title of the novel is *About a Boy*, the reader will soon discover that this book is really **about two boys**: the real boy Marcus Brewer and the man who, like Peter Pan, has never really grown up: Will Freeman.
As a boy, Will's position at school had been similar to Marcus's. He, too, had been an outsider. Nobody at school had had a father who "had made his money in quite the same way" (p. 6). But Will had not been "a nerdy kid with the wrong trainers". He had worn the right clothes, had the right haircut "and he'd successfully avoided being bullied by bullying furiously and enthusiastically." (p. 125)
Paradoxically, 12-year-old Marcus, a serious boy who wears thick glasses, is bullied at school and knows nothing about the latest kids' fashions or trends in pop music, seems older than 36-year-old Will, who reads the right magazines, always has the right clothes and hairstyle and (like many normal kids) has no worries except possible boredom.
Marcus has his mother to look after him: she tells him what to do. Will has Santa Claus (and the money he provides) to look after him: the glossy magazines he reads tell him what to buy, where to go and what to do in his endless free time.
Both of them share the experience of "growing up with a batty [= crazy] parent" (p. 126), and Will realizes that he should use his own experience to help Marcus. But at this stage, halfway through the book, Will Freeman still lacks **commitment** (see below).
Like Peter Pan, Will inhabits an unreal world of his own. He has "spent his whole life avoiding real stuff. [...] Santa Claus, whose existence most adults had real cause to doubt, bought him everything he wore and ate and drank

and sat on and lived in; [...] reality was not in his genes." (p. 104) Early on in the book, Will tells himself: "You didn't have to have a life of your own any more; you could just peek over the fence at other people's lives as lived in newspapers and EastEnders and films and exquisitely sad jazz or tough rap songs." (pp. 6–7) Will does not have to face real life.

Marcus has to face "real stuff" at school and at home every day: his mother's attempted suicide, the fear that she may try to kill herself again, trying without much success to keep out of the other kids' way at school. He is being forced to grow up fast but does not know how to cope with his problems at home and at school.

Will is "one of life's visitors; he didn't like to be visited." (p. 93) This underlines Will's lack of commitment. You need commitment to have a job, to start a family, to do anything that might make you an interesting person. When Will asks Marcus: "What do you think school's for?", Marcus touches a raw nerve: "Getting a job. [...] You could have left school when you were about six or seven. [...] Why did you go to school? [...] If I knew I wasn't going to get a job, I wouldn't bother." (p. 98) Will tells him to shut up, quickly changing the subject. This reaction shows that Marcus realizes what a pointless life Will leads (see "The point", p. 83 below) and that Will is sensitive to this fact.

Fiona is quick to put her finger on one childish aspect of Will's character: his tendency to tell lies and make things up. Talking of Will's imaginary son Ned, she says: "The point is, Marcus, that Will left school a long time ago. He should have grown out of making people up by now." (p. 170)

Will's financial independence frees him from dependence on other people – including work colleagues and employers. But this freedom also means that he has never had to grow up. At the age of 36 he is, as Rachel puts it on p. 210, "a sort of blank – you didn't do anything, you weren't passionate about anything, you didn't seem to have much to say – and then when you said you had a kid – [...] I thought, I've got this guy all wrong." At the beginning of the book he is proud of organizing his empty days around half-hour units of time (many of which, such as "doing a quick crossword on the toilet" [p. 71]), may strike the reader as fairly empty in themselves).

Marcus's childhood is over at the age of twelve, when his mother tries to commit suicide. He realizes that unless he gets more help from "the woman under the coat" (p. 40) he will "have to be his own mother" (p. 119) even though he does not know how to do this.

6.5 Coolness

Despite being a positive synonym for words like "trendy", "fashionable", "with-it" or simply "fantastic" in the English (or for that matter German) language, the adjective "cool" still has the negative meaning of 'unfeeling', 'distanced', 'cold and unemotional'.

Will's coolness (in the positive sense of the word) is quickly identified when we first meet him (pp. 5 and 6). He is "sub-zero". There is plenty of humour in this description of Will but the reader cannot help feeling that a person whose highest ethical belief is that it is wrong to lie about oneself in questionnaires must have a fairly shallow personality. "He would die of hypothermia!" can be seen not so much as a cause for self-congratulation by Will but as a warning that a cool life without deep emotional entanglements is perhaps not such a good idea.
Quite late in the novel, Will remembers a phrase which his ex-girlfriend Jessica had used while telling him what a useless, meaningless, pointless person he was: someone who could have done something meaningful with her (i.e. start a family). She had recommended him to "*sprinkle some salt on the ice* [...] by having a relationship that meant something, and maybe a family." (p. 220)

6.6 Commitment

Commitment – and Will's lack of it – is a theme which occurs early on in the novel in Chapter 2, and is seen in the novel as the opposite of **coolness**.
Will's friends John and Christine are certainly committed: they are married and have two children, Barney, aged two, and Imogen, only a week old. When Christine brings in the new baby and asks Will if he has any desire for a family of his own yet, he replies "Not yet" while thinking that he "would rather eat one of Barney's dirty nappies" (p. 8), a good example of the contrast between actual dialogue and what the speaker is thinking.
When John and Christine invite him to become Imogen's godfather – a relatively lightweight commitment after all – he declines with thanks, admitting almost proudly that he has no "hidden depths", that he really is "this shallow" (p. 9).
Fiona's commitment to her vegetarian, "think-for-yourself-don't-be-a-sheep" lifestyle is clear from Chapter 3 onwards, and is the main obstacle to Marcus's assimilation at school: "if he wanted to do anything that any of the other kids spent their time doing, he had to argue with her for hours. He usually lost, and she was so good at arguing that he felt good about losing." (p. 13)
Will rejects commitment completely because he believes that deep involvement with one's partner or other people's lives and problems is what makes people unhappy and miserable. This is something he wishes to avoid at all costs. He fails to realize that there can be no happiness without the contrast of unhappiness. No deep positive feelings without the risk of deep negative feelings. No depth at all, in fact, if all you do is float on the surface of life, refusing to become involved in it.
Fairly late in the novel, when he expresses a wish for "a life of his own" and searches desperately for some aspect of his empty life that would make him

"interesting" to Rachel, he realizes that only commitment, only involvement in real life, can make him an interesting person.
Will's commitment begins with Marcus, who literally blackmails his way into Will's flat and life with the statement: "You haven't got a kid, have you?" [...] "I'll do you a deal. I won't say anything to my mum if you go out with her." (pp. 91–93) Gradually, Will finds himself "working Marcus's visits into the fabric of his day" and he decides to help the boy to cope with some of his problems. He can help him with the external aspects of life. Halfway through the book Will at last realizes that Marcus needs "help to be a kid, not an adult". He cannot tell Marcus "how to grow up, or how to cope with a suicidal mother [...] but he could certainly tell him that Kurt Cobain didn't play for Manchester United, and for a twelve-year-old boy attending a comprehensive school at the end of 1993, that was maybe the most important information of all." (p. 147)
Will's commitment to other people and life in general finally comes when he falls in love with Rachel.

6.7 Gender conflict – *Men Are from Mars, Women Are from Venus*

This is the title of a very successful and important book by John Gray published in 1992. It deals with the relationships between the sexes and argues that men and women are completely different creatures from different planets or, rather, that they have different ways of looking at the same thing. This leads to problems of communication between the sexes and to the break-up of relationships unless each side is prepared to see the other's point of view.
As a novelist, Nick Hornby is deeply concerned with "male problems". Women – whether feminists like it or not – are much more committed to caring for a family. There are clear references to this in *About a Boy*. When Marcus talks to Ellie about his mum's attempted suicide, she tells him that he would have been all right if Fiona had killed herself (p. 182). Marcus objects to that view calling into account his mum's responsibility and at last he wins the argument.
The message is clear. Women *are* from Venus. Will indirectly recognizes this fact when he wonders, during his first conversation with Fiona alone: "What planet did this woman live on? She was so unworldly that she seemed to him to be an unlikely suicidal depressive" (p. 131). But Will's world is, of course, not the real world either.
Because they come from different planets, Will finds it very difficult to discuss Fiona's problems seriously with her. When they are having a meal in a restaurant after Rachel has failed to turn up for a woman-to-woman discussion in Chapter 32, Will realizes with near-frustration that he will never find a way into the conversation which they must have "while he was stuck with

his brain and his vocabulary and his personality. He kept feeling as though he were on the verge of saying something proper and serious and useful; but then he ended up thinking, Oh fuck it, say something stupid instead." (p. 243)

Obviously he must change his brain, his vocabulary and, most of all, his personality. At last he says: "I want to help, but I know I won't be able to. I haven't got the answers to anything." Fiona reminds him that this is exactly "what men think". And she explains: "That unless you've got some answer, unless you can say 'Oh, I know this bloke in Essex Road who can fix that for you', then it's not worth bothering." (pp. 243–244) This is exactly what Will thinks, and (humour here) he admits to himself that he "had spent half the evening trying to think of the name of the bloke in Essex Road, metaphorically speaking." (p. 244)

This comment marks a change in his relationship to Fiona, perhaps even in his own personality. Will realizes that he can help Fiona without knowing the answers to her problems. He just listens sympathetically to a woman's outpourings, nodding and asking pertinent questions. He has done this many times before, but always with the ulterior motive of getting a woman into bed. This time he only wants Fiona to feel better. His character is developing in a positive direction at last. He is thinking more about others, less about himself.

6.8 Sincerity, engagement and vulnerability

Many intelligent adult readers will sympathize with Fiona's alternative lifestyle: these readers will include single mothers, feminists, environmentalists, vegetarians, aroma therapists, ageing hippies etc. For their ideas and ideals are Fiona's ideas and ideals. The problem – Marcus's problem – is that she imposes her sincere beliefs on her son.

Many people will agree with her views on individuality, on not being a sheep ("Sheep," says Marcus in the trainer shop: "Baaaaa." – p. 111), but this is no help to Marcus. He is weird because his mother is weird. She manipulates her son by arguing with him about issues such as vegetarianism, music and fashion until he agrees with her: "except he hadn't agreed really; he'd just lost the arguments." (p. 121) She thinks she is teaching Marcus to think for himself, but he recognizes that this kind of argument is manipulation: "But all that happens," he tells his mother in frustration, "is we have an argument and I lose".

What makes Fiona and Marcus different from Will or Ellie is their **sincerity**. Marcus realizes that although in discussions at school everyone agrees that smoking is bad, many kids still smoke. He sees that most people

> "thought one thing and did another. In Marcus's house it was different. They decided what was bad and then they never touched it or did it again. […]
> But of all the things that made him different, he could see this was the most important. It was why he wore clothes that other kids laughed at – because […] they'd [he and Fiona] agreed that fashion was stupid – and why he listened to music that was old-fashioned [...] – because they'd had this talk about modern pop music, and they'd agreed it was just a way for record companies to make a lot of money. It was why he wasn't allowed to play violent computer games, or eat hamburgers […] he'd agreed with her about all of it, except he hadn't agreed really; he'd just lost the arguments." (pp. 120–121)

Will already knows that sincerity is the quickest way to unhappiness. Deep feelings make people **vulnerable**, which is why Will avoids them. When Fiona plays the piano and sings her seventies songs (p. 89), she really *means* them. She is inside them. Marcus joins in and they close their eyes as they sing: a sure sign of sincerity. Perhaps Will closes his eyes, but for a different reason: "He knew […] that singing round the piano with a depressive hippy and her weirdo son wouldn't kill him […] but he didn't *feel* it. He couldn't do anything with these people after all […]. He'd been stupid to think there was anything here for him." (p. 90) Will's ego speaks:

> "You had to be engaged to be a vegetarian, you had to be engaged to sing 'Both Sides Now' with your eyes closed; when it came down to it, you had to be engaged to be a mother. He wasn't much bothered either way about anything, and that, he knew, would guarantee him a long and depression-free life. He'd made a big mistake thinking that good works were a way forward for him. They weren't. They drove you mad. Fiona did good works and they had driven her mad: she was vulnerable, messed-up, inadequate." (p. 90)

On the other hand, Marcus's sincerity in his feelings towards Ellie and his lack of self-pity (p. 205) almost make Will want to hug him.
One reason why Will avoids commitment and sincerity is because it would make him vulnerable. In his shallow dealings with other people, Will is an emotional coward. He is afraid of being hurt.
Early in the novel he obviously prefers the idea of a "long and depression-free life". Only later does he discover that it is worth risking the deep disappointments and pain which deep emotions like love cannot be separated from.

6.9 Sex and love

Although Will has had plenty of sex in his life, he has never been in love until he meets Rachel in Chapter 24. For Will, who always uses a condom, sex, although he explains to Marcus that it is "kind of a big deal" (p. 190), has always been "some sort of fantastic carnal alternative to drink, drugs and a great night out, but nothing much more than that" (p. 228). There is, of course,

heavy irony in this description of Will's attitude to sex. No sign of emotion, no commitment, not even the romance of the serial pulp-fiction novelette! But after having had sex with Rachel, Will "couldn't ever remember feeling so happy." (p. 228) He is discovering love as opposed to sex.
It is falling in love with Rachel that marks the final change in Will's shallow, egoistic personality. Because love (not just sex) involves a **commitment** of the kind he has been avoiding throughout all his life.
Marcus develops a kind of pre-pubescent love (we would call it a "crush") for Ellie which corresponds in its emotional intensity to Will's feelings for Rachel. When Will asks Marcus what he feels about Ellie, Marcus says: "I want to be with her all the time [...]. I want Ellie to myself. And I want to tell her things first, before I tell anyone, even you or Mum. And I don't want her to have another boyfriend. If I could have all those things, I wouldn't mind if I touched her or not." (p. 191)
Alone in bed that night, Will agrees with Marcus that "he'd settle for the less and the more that Marcus wanted". This is a desire for true love, not just for sex. And love is impossible without **vulnerability**: letting another person into your life and sharing life with all its problems can lead to unhappiness, but it is an unhappiness that can be diminished by being shared.

6.10 Drugs

The theme of drugs is not a main topic of this novel. Drugs are treated in a matter-of-fact way in the same category as alcohol and nicotine. In any case, the smoking of marihuana by adults in private is no longer a crime in Britain. Taking drugs is, in Will's eyes, part of being cool, part of modern life. He thinks about his own boring youth and comes to the rather cynical conclusion: "It was no wonder young people were turning to crime and drugs and prostitution. [...] because they were on the menu now, an exciting, colourful and tasty new range of options that he had been denied [when he himself was young]" (p. 75). When he explains the pictures of jazz musicians on his walls to Marcus, Will says: "I like their music and they're cool." When Marcus asks him why they are cool, he replies: "I don't know. Because they took drugs and died, probably." (p. 97)
Apart from marihuana, the only other drugs mentioned are Ecstasy (p. 5 in connection with the coolness questionnaire) and "magic mushrooms" (p. 221) (a hallucinogenic drug obtained from dried mushrooms and containing psilocybin. Its effects resemble a shorter-acting LSD trip).

6.11 "The point" – the meaning of life

Few phrases occur as often in the novel as the words "the point" – the reason for doing things, or, in a deeper sense, the meaning of life. We can imagine

Fiona asking herself: "What's the point in living?" when she decides to commit suicide.
Will reacts violently and allergically throughout the novel to any mention of "the point" because he knows deep inside himself that his life has *no* point. "You couldn't have a talk about life, and especially about the possibility of ending it, without bringing up the fucking point, and Will just couldn't see one." But he realizes that "Telling someone like Fiona that there was no point was more or less the same as killing her off" (p. 221).
For a while his imaginary son Ned is the point of being a member of SPAT. Lying about Ned – and putting off the time when he cannot avoid showing him to Suzie any longer – is difficult, but, having invented him, Will cannot kill Ned off tragically or pack him off to his imaginary ex-wife Paula because "he wouldn't be a single father any more. He'd lose the point of himself somehow." (p. 45) As Will is pretty pointless anyway, this would be no great loss. We smile, as we are perhaps intended to do.
So one of the main themes of the novel is Will's search for a point that would justify his life. But his life at the beginning of the book is pointless, as he himself knows, and he gradually realizes that he will have to change his life in order to find this point.
Marcus often misses **the point** of jokes or sarcasm because he is a serious boy who takes what people say quite literally. But he is quick to see that Will's comforting words at the hospital after Fiona's attempted suicide ("She'll be OK", p. 59) are "not the point". She may try again. So the point for Marcus soon becomes making sure his mother does not try to kill herself again by trying to bring Will and Fiona together.
For men, of course, everything has to have a point. There always has to be some bloke in Essex Road who can fix things. Marcus soon becomes the point in Will's life. In Chapter 16 he finds it easy to work Marcus's visits "into the fabric of his day. This wasn't difficult to do, since the fabric of his day was tatty and filled with any number of large and accommodating holes." Will realizes that he "was serving some purpose in the kid's life at the moment". This is a new role for Will. More and more he feels the need for a point in his own life. Although Rachel tells him: "You don't need a point" (p. 225), she goes on to say that, for most people, "the point is something to do with work, or kids, or family, or whatever. But you don't have any of that. There's nothing between you and despair" (p. 226), which makes it more important to Will than ever before to find a point to his life. Rachel suggests that looking forward to the next Nirvana album or the next episode of a crime series like *NYPD Blue* provide Will's life with some kind of point, but at this stage in his search for himself Will clearly does not think this is enough. "'That's the point? *NYPD Blue?* Jesus.' It was worse than he thought." (p. 226)
Waiting for the next episode in a TV crime series surely cannot be the meaning of life, but Rachel goes on to admit that looking forward to what is just

around the corner saved her from suicide. She tells Will that Marcus "adores" him – something which had never occurred to Will, perhaps because he is not very familiar with deep feelings. But even at this stage in the book (p. 225), Will can still say: "He's still not the point", though the reader does not really believe him.

6.12 Suicide and death

Suicide, or attempted suicide (parasuicide), is a major theme in the book. It is what brings Marcus and Will together in the first place. One of the main reasons why Marcus visits Will so often is to avoid going straight home from school and perhaps finding his mother has tried to kill herself again.
In her suicide note, Fiona produces the standard arguments of the depressive: "I'm tired and bored and the party's gone on too long and I want to go home. I feel flat and there doesn't seem to be anything to look forward to, so I'd rather call it a day." (p. 65)
Fiona's depression and the risk of another suicide attempt add to Marcus's problems at school. He feels responsible for his mother, taking over a role normally belonging to a partner, and his naive attempts at matchmaking are aimed at finding a "replacement partner" for his mother to give more security to the family unit.
The reasons for Kurt Cobain's suicide – and attempted suicide before that – are not given. Katrina suggests that he was "unhappy [...]. Drugs? A bad childhood? Pressure? That sort of thing, anyway." (p. 259) But its effects on Ellie certainly influence the action of the novel.
Another suicide by a pop singer which Will remembers well is mentioned on pages 245 and 246: Marvin Gaye, who killed himself on 1st April 1984 when Will was twenty-six "and still of an age when things like that meant something: he probably sang Marvin Gaye songs with his eyes closed when he was twenty-six." 36-year-old Will denies that such deaths mean anything to him now. "The only consequence of Kurt Cobain's death as far as he was concerned was that *Nevermind* would sound a lot cooler." (p. 246) Even Will's cynicism at this late stage in the novel is counterbalanced by the thought that he might have showed more true emotion ten years before.
Will's father, a sad and disappointed man, must be included in this category, too. His failure as a song-writer to repeat the success of "Santa's Super Sleigh" led to a feeling of general failure and to a slower, more indirect form of suicide: "So what if Charles Freeman had killed himself with expensive malt whisky, and Fiona had tried to kill herself with National Health tranquillizers?" (p. 126)
Even level-headed Rachel admits to having thought about suicide a few years before, when she was really low, but says that she always found reasons for putting it off: "Maybe tomorrow, but not today. And after a few weeks [...] I knew I was never going to do it [...] because I didn't want to miss out. I don't

mean that life was great [...] [but] there were always one or two things that seemed unfinished, things I wanted to follow through." (p. 227)
Fiona must have similar reasons for going on living, but perhaps she is not getting the breaks that Rachel gets. She also suffers from depression, an ill ness which gives people who suffer from it a pessimistic outlook on life.
Death also appears in other forms in the novel. There is, of course, Dead Duck Day. Ironically, this is the first time that Marcus has ever succeeded in doing something he has been trying to do: to hit a duck with a piece of bread.
Will's defence of Marcus – accused by the park-keeper of deliberately killing the duck – marks the beginning of their friendship, and during the embarrassing confrontation between Will and Suzie at Fiona's Christmas party, mention of the "killing" causes Suzie and Fiona to collapse into hysterical laughter (Marcus's father, Lindsey and her mother are less impressed: "The audience on the sofa looked appalled" [p. 170] – but perhaps this is because they come from a different world: Cambridge). The embarrassment is forgotten, and Will sits down again.
Death appears again when Katrina, on the way to Royston, says that Ellie is, figuratively, "killing" her by the way she behaves. Will is perhaps reminded of Dracula stories when he thinks of parents as "the Undead" on p. 258: "Ellie was killing Katrina, and Marcus was killing Fiona, and they would go on killing them for years and years. They were the Undead. They couldn't live, not properly, and they couldn't die; all they could do was sit in a stranger's car and laugh about it. And people like Jessica had the nerve to tell him that he was missing out!"
And, of course, "Killing Me Softly" is one of Fiona's favourite songs.

6.13 Individualism and bullying

In the animal kingdom, outsiders are mercilessly excluded from the herd. The same behaviour can be seen in the human world. Ellie is just as much an outsider as Marcus, but she has better back-up: her anger at life, her reputation as a bad girl, her friends. Her mother Katrina is almost normal by comparison with Fiona, although she admits that she has lost control of her daughter. Fiona only begins to lose control of Marcus at the end of the book, and, as Marcus's only back-up person at the beginning, she is best described in Marcus's own word: "crap". She has him firmly under control until he gets to know Will and Ellie better, but because she is an outsider in a hostile world herself, she is the person who does most to prevent Marcus's integration.
Will is right in the methods he uses to help Marcus to be a kid and she (despite the rightness of many of her alternative views) is wrong. Marcus needs to become more like a sheep and "less visible" in his environment.
But when talking about right and wrong, we must remember the apparent paradox "it's no good being right if everybody else is wrong".

The author is not encouraging young people to submit unconditionally and uncritically to peer-group pressure at school. He shows how the boy can be helped to survive life among the "sheep" until he can decide for himself which way to go. The book ends with Marcus far more in control of his own situation: he has lost the 'old' Marcus but is on his way to finding his new self, and Fiona, because her son is easier to handle now that he has more friends, is happier and less depressed without knowing why.
Will knows why, but he is wise enough not to tell her.

6.14 The importance of music in the novel

Music plays an important part in *About a Boy*. Fiona is a music therapist and Marcus is given some sheet music at Christmas as "a gentle and very dull maternal reminder [...] that [he] had given up on his lessons some time ago" (p. 162). Marcus sings to himself (pp. 14–15, 39), but they are the wrong songs – the songs his mum likes, for example: "a Joni Mitchell one about a taxi" (p. 39). When one of the school bullies asks him: "Who's your favourite rapper? Tupac? Warren G?", Marcus knows the names but dare not answer or "he'd be sunk" (p. 29).
It is Will who introduces Marcus to Nirvana as well as giving him a Kurt Cobain T-shirt and a vinyl copy of Nirvana's album *Nevermind* for Christmas (p. 96). In conversation with Ellie and Zoe (p. 149), Marcus says: "I don't know what I think of grunge. [...] It's a bit of a racket, but it's got a good beat, and the picture on the cover is very interesting." These naive comments make the girls laugh. They ask him his name, and he has the longest conversation he has ever had with anyone at school for weeks as a result. "He didn't think he'd ever like [grunge] as much as he liked Joni or Bob [Dylan] or Mozart", but it is Will's choice of music, not his mother's, which improves his school situation, and Marcus's own tastes have changed by the last page of the book, where he states: "I bloody hate Joni Mitchell." As with the trainers which he buys him, Will points Marcus in the right musical direction, again helping him to become "less visible" at school.
Fiona would never have done this. She has brought her son up on her own 60s and 70s hippy music. The words of the songs which Fiona sings are as important as the music itself. She sings with her eyes closed, and this gesture is a symbol throughout the novel of **sincerity** (see p. 81). "Fiona meant it. She meant 'Knocking On Heaven's Door', and then she meant 'Fire And Rain', and then she meant 'Both Sides Now'. There was nothing between her and the songs; she was inside them. She even closed her eyes when she was singing." (p. 89) Unfortunately, Fiona's taste in music has not changed since her younger days. Her opinion of modern pop music, expressed in one of her "arguments" with Marcus (which she always wins), is that it is all about making money. This may disqualify the music by Fiona's moral standards but her

views will not help Marcus to fit in better at school. Fiona's taste in music (as in several other things) is shown in a negative light when she naively admits, of Kurt Cobain: "I'd never heard of him before Christmas [...] but he was quite a big deal, wasn't he?" (p. 259) A good example of the author's use of irony in view of the fact that he states, through Will on p. 147, that knowing "that Kurt Cobain didn't play for Manchester United" was "for a twelve-year-old boy attending a comprehensive school at the end of 1993 [...] maybe the most important information of all."

Will's taste in music has kept pace with the times. Marcus is surprised at "the flash hi-fi, the hundreds of CDs and thousands of records and tapes, the black and white photos of people playing saxophones" (p. 96) which he discovers on his first visit to Will's flat. When Marcus asks why Will has pictures of Charlie Parker and Chet Baker on his walls, Will admits to liking their music and finding them cool. When asked why he finds them cool, he replies: "Because they took drugs and died, probably." But this is just the kind of flip answer we would expect Will to give. After all, music has shaped his life: in the form of "Santa's Super Sleigh". And after Kurt Cobain's suicide, Will admits to the deep feelings aroused in him, in younger years, by music: "Will wondered whether Marcus had ever sat in his room listening to *Nevermind* in the same way that Will had sat in his room listening to the first Clash album." (p. 259) Even at the age of 36, Will is still moved by "exquisitely sad jazz or tough rap songs" (p. 7). He admits that, ten years previously, "he probably sang Marvin Gaye songs with his eyes closed when he was twenty-six." Marvin Gaye, the black soul singer, was shot by his own father in a domestic argument at the age of 44 in 1984. In those days Will had still thought that such deaths *meant* something. "Now he knew that pop stars committing suicide were all grist to the mill, and the only consequence of Kurt Cobain's death as far as he was concerned was that *Nevermind* would sound a lot cooler". Even as late in the novel as this, we still see a rather cynical Will, though he has let the world into his life far enough to express his worry that Marcus and Ellie "would think it all meant something" (all quotes from p. 246).

Then there is the question of how far the extremely popular, but musically probably worthless song "Santa's Super Sleigh" is responsible for Will's failure to develop as a person. Certainly Will blames its success for his father's failure as a musician, his alcoholism and ultimate death. Although it is Will's only source of income, the song is a frequent source of psychological pain to him (p. 123). Perhaps he should have decided when much younger to donate the song royalties to charity and started his own life much sooner. But that would have been too idealistic – too much like hard work for Will the Hedonist, who has more opportunities than most people to pursue the "pleasure principle" (the *Lustprinzip* first formulated by the German philosopher G.Th. Fechner [1801–87] and later expanded by Sigmund Freud): the human tendency to seek pleasure and avoid pain.

The Film

"Who said: 'No man is an island'?" These are almost the first words spoken on the film sound-track, in the form of a "Who-said-it?" question on the TV quiz show *Countdown* which Will Freeman is watching as the film starts.
No words could summarize the message of the book better. Will, however, does not share this opinion, and his impatient gesture in switching off the TV at this point demonstrates this all too clearly. But he is wrong. Just as his answer to the "Who-said-it?" question is wrong. The quotation is not from the pop musician John Bon Jovi but from the deeply-religious Elizabethan metaphysical poet John Donne (1572–1631). It is a passage at the beginning of Meditation 17 in his *Devotions* which he wrote during a dangerous illness in the winter of 1623. This well-known quotation (spelling and language have been modernized) goes:

> "No man is an island, entire of itself, every man is a piece of the Continent, a part of the Main[land]; if a clod be washed away by the sea, Europe is the less, as well as if a promontory were, as well as if a manor [= group] of thy [= your] friends or of thine [= your] own [family] were; any man's death diminishes me, because I am involved in Mankind. And therefore never send to know for whom the bell tolls. It tolls for thee [= you]."

John Donne was brought up as a Catholic in the days when such "old believers" were still much persecuted for their beliefs. He studied at Oxford at an early age to avoid having to become a member of the Protestant Church of England (until the 19th century, only Anglicans were allowed to study at Oxford or Cambridge) and went on to study law at Lincoln's Inn (London) in 1592. He practised law for four years and lived a reckless, hedonistic life. His marriage to Ann More brought many years of poverty during which he wrote some of his most passionate love poems (only published after his death). He became a Church of England priest in 1615 and obtained the important post of Dean of St. Paul's Cathedral in London in 1621. His sermons place him among the greatest orators of his century, and his passionate poems of love and hate, violent, tender or abusive, give him a unique position among English poets.
But what is the relevance of this quotation to Hornby's novel and the film version? Apart from being a much-used warning to those who think that other people's problems are not theirs as well as to those who don't prepare for death, it has provided the title of at least two major works of 20th century literature: Johannes Mario Simmel's *Niemand ist eine Insel* (1975) and, perhaps better known (and certainly better as literature), Ernest Hemingway's novel

For Whom the Bell Tolls (1941), which is set in the turmoil of the Spanish Civil War of the 1930s.

Although Hornby never actually uses the words “No man is an island” in the book, the film begins with these words, and they are repeated at the end. In the use of the word “island” there is also an echo of the Simon and Garfunkel 60s hit “I am an Island”, where the self-sufficient loner, safe in his “fortress deep and mighty” rejects love because of the pain it has caused: “I touch no one and no one touches me / I am a rock, I am an island / And a rock feels no pain, and an island never cries.” Like the Donne quotation above, these words could well be applied to Will Freeman at the beginning of the film.

Similarities with the Book

The film (directed by Paul and Chris Weitz; GB/USA 2002) sticks very closely to the action of the book. The location is the same. The film was made in the London Borough of Highbury. With the exception of Marcus (played in the film by twelve-year-old Nicholas Hoult), the characters are all as the reader of the book would imagine them: the egocentric Will Freeman played by the cool and attractive Hugh Grant; the ageing hippy Fiona complete with hand-knitted pullovers, scarf and Lapland cap played by Toni Collette; beautiful Rachel played by beautiful Rachel Weisz; Ellie the punk, complete with nose piercing.

The film makes much use of the internal monologue of the book (the actual thoughts of the protagonists). This double, voice-over narration is one of the film’s most interesting aspects. It often produces a comic contrast between what Will or Marcus says and what he actually thinks. The fact that both main protagonists are male means that we are only given an insight into the thoughts of the male characters, emphasizing Hornby’s interest in male problems perhaps even more than the book itself does.

Important Differences and Changes

The Marcus of the film is not quite the Marcus of the novel. He does not wear glasses. Despite his home-made haircut and clothes, “cheeky” rather than “geeky”, would be a better description of the boy who plays this role. The film industry obviously required a more attractive child actor. Marcus’s cheekiness increases as the film proceeds.

The film begins with Will, not Marcus. This enables the basic “No man is an island” theme to be introduced right at the start. In the second scene, Marcus is seen cleaning his hamster’s cage, though we know from the book that he has never had a pet or looked after anything.

There is no break-up between Fiona and her boyfriend at the beginning of the film. We see her in her depressed state right from the start, crying as she tries to make breakfast for her son.
The incident with the headmistress, Mrs Morrison (Chapter 19), is left out, so the social stigma of playing truant from school is avoided. In the film we have a comic scene where Marcus, listening to his new CD, walks down the school corridor behind Ellie and other older kids with his eyes closed, singing: "Uh, Ah, shake your ass!"
There is no reference to Kurt Cobain or Nirvana in the film, so the suicide aspect is restricted to Fiona's attempt to kill herself. The music which Marcus listens to on his portable CD player is standard rap (particularly Mystikal) and the entire musical score of the movie was composed by the British indie (= independent) songwriter Badly Drawn Boy. Even the relatively harmless drug-taking aspects of the book are left out of the film apart from occasional references in the dialogue.
When Fiona discovers that Marcus has been going round to Will's flat regularly, she takes him straight to the restaurant where Will is having dinner with Christine (John's wife from Chapter 2). The confrontation between Fiona and Will and suggestions of "child molestation" are thus made public – and much more embarrassing for Will – in the film while, in the book, the scene takes place in Will's flat. Christine and a waitress give additional comments while the other diners look on. This is a much more powerful scene in the film than the (still powerful) passage in the novel.
When Will hears the song "Santa's Super Sleigh" for the first time that year in a supermarket on November 19th, he has a sudden vision of his dead father which parallels Marcus's vision of his mother in Regent's Park on Dead Duck Day. This is a very emotional moment for Will, though it is easily missed as it only lasts a split second on the screen. Later in the film, after Will has confessed to Rachel that Marcus is not his son, Will takes out a CD labelled *One Hit Wonders* (the title of a newspaper article in the book) and plays his father's song. We are left with a feeling of sadness at the figure of a very depressed Will lying face down on the carpet, perhaps paying homage to his dead parent despite his hatred of the song.
Marcus and Ellie's journey to Cambridge and the incident at the music shop in Royston, the scene at the police station where the adult parents confront each other and Marcus's conversation with his father Clive in Cambridge (Chapters 31 to 35) are all left out. Perhaps because they are too socially critical. So there is no evidence of Clive having a "big think" about his life. He is only seen at Fiona's Christmas party, a smiling and slightly vacuous figure.
These five chapters are replaced in the film by Marcus's participation in his school's rock concert where, despite warnings from Ellie and others, he decides to sing one of his mum's favourite songs, "Killing Me Softly", which Fiona sings on p. 90 in the book and also earlier on in the film. Will finds out

about the concert from Fiona, whom he embarrassingly confronts at a SPAT meeting, begging her not to try and kill herself again. Another comic scene not based on the book.

They drive quickly round to the school. Fiona insists that Marcus has a right to express himself through singing, but Will's highly relevant comment is: "He's not expressing *himself*, he's expressing *you*!" Will is determined to try and stop Marcus's potentially "suicidal" performance and, rushing into the school hall, he suddenly sees Rachel (who has been absent from the action in the film since Will's "confession" at the restaurant) in the audience. Her son Ali is performing virtuoso acrobatics on the stage to a red-hot rap number announced as "Murder for Life" by The Death-penalty Crew.

Marcus's turn comes and Will tries to persuade him not to go on the stage: "Nothing you do will make your mum happy," he tells Marcus. "You have to make yourself happy." But Marcus overcomes his stage fright and the curtain opens to reveal a very small boy alone on a very large stage (his accompanist on the recorder has already abandoned him off-stage, returning the £5 which Marcus had paid him rather than commit social suicide). "This is for my mum," announces Marcus, and begins to sing.

The embarrassing situation is saved by Will, who suddenly appears on the stage playing a guitar he has borrowed. Ellie, in the audience, slaps a boy who shouts a rude comment and is cheered for her action. The mood of the audience changes. Will takes over the singing and becomes as unstoppable as Fiona, in the book, had been in her defence of her son at Royston police station.

At last we see a committed Will – "singing with my eyes shut" is his voice-over comment on his final acceptance of commitment. Will, who throughout the book and the film showed great fear of embarrassment, now publicly makes a fool of himself. This demands the same kind of courage which Marcus, who knows that he is "crap at drama" (p. 12), needs in order to appear on the school stage as a solo singer. The film thus strongly emphasizes two examples of love that are not present in the scenes in the book (Royston and Cambridge) which they replace: Marcus's love for his mother and Will's commitment to Marcus.

Having accepted Marcus's contribution to the concert, the audience now tries to boo Will off the stage. An apple, thrown by someone in the audience at Will's head, is frozen in mid air while we hear Will express these thoughts. There was a similar scene at the beginning of the film where a football was stopped just before it hit Marcus on the head in order to allow Marcus to make a statement about the "shit time" he is having at school.

After the concert, Fiona even suggests taking Marcus to McDonald's for a hamburger feast. This gives Marcus, in the film, the chance to show generosity (and a certain forgiveness) towards his vegetarian mother by refusing her kind offer.

The theme of Clive as a "failed father" who has "missed his moment" with Marcus but is thinking of having a second try at fatherhood with a child from Lindsey is also left out of the film. Like Ellie's anti-authoritarian protest gesture in Royston, it would have provided an unnecessary complication of the basic plot of the film.
The film draws to an end on the same optimistic note as the book. The scene is a Christmas party the following year at Will's flat. At first the viewer might think that Will is alone, but Rachel moves into the picture and kisses him. The camera then shows Marcus and Ali. Ellie and Fiona are heard working in the kitchen with a much more suitable potential partner for Fiona: a middle-aged gentleman with a beard who was seen earlier in the film working in an Amnesty International office where Will seems to have spent one day of his working life, as a volunteer, and whom Will has invited over "on the spur of the moment" to Christmas dinner. Thus the optimistic view of the future takes in even Fiona at the end of the film.
The message from Will at the beginning of this scene is that *every* man is an island, but that these islands form parts of island chains, connected under water to each other. Everybody can thus be an individual without losing contact with the people around him or her: a compromise between Will's former isolation and Marcus's insistence on "back-up".
The film ends with a smiling Marcus quoting the words which, according to Will, were spoken by John Bon Jovi: "No man is an island."

When interviewed by *The Guardian* about the changes in the plot at the end of the film, Nick Hornby said that the ending was "true to the spirit of the book; it really, really works". The film-makers, he continues "have chosen a path that I didn't choose, but now wish I had".
It is always easier to improve something which already exists. The ending of the film is certainly more satisfying than the ending in the book. All the main protagonists are brought together at a Christmas party, illustrating and vindicating Marcus's "human pyramid" theory. They are all enjoying themselves, and the presence of the bearded Amnesty International worker (who has no idea why he was suddenly invited to Will's party) gives the audience some hope that even depressive Fiona might still find a partner.
The introduction of the "no-man-is-an-island" motif is a stroke of genius, blending in exactly with the main theme of the book and underlining it even more firmly than the novel itself.
The film-makers have also introduced things which make the film funnier: with the exception of Suzie, the women at the first SPAT meeting are deliberately unattractive. This makes Will's search for "beautiful single mothers" appear even crazier than it is 'unethical'.
During the SPAT picnic, the baguette which Marcus throws at the duck is turned into one of Fiona's heavy home-made loaves. When Will says how

good it looks, Marcus responds: "It isn't good, it's *healthy*", thus making fun of the alternative lifestyle he is forced to share with his mother. A piece of added humour not present in the novel.

One tiny but very significant difference between the novel and the film is used with great effect to emphasize one of Will's greatest weaknesses. On p. 201, when Rachel is explaining why Ali is so upset about her relationships with men, particularly her last partner, Ali says: "He was a weirdo", which does not mean much. In the film Ali says: "He was a **liar**." This applies directly to Will, and Ali's dramatic outburst in the film may influence Will to abandon lying as a strategy. In the book Will himself realizes that "he was not, as he had always previously thought, a good liar. He was an enthusiastic liar, certainly, but enthusiasm was not the same thing as efficacy" (pp. 187–188). Ali's altered statement about someone else draws Will's attention to one of his own main failings. This is a good example of how, with the benefit of hindsight, the film scriptwriter can 'improve' on the original text of the novel by changing one single word.

The inclusion of the rock concert in the film emphasizes an element of courage in Marcus that is absent from the book, but, for the other characters, the film still contains all the basic themes of the book: selfishness, lack of commitment, helplessness, dysfunctional family units, love leading to commitment. The only major omission by comparison with the novel is the development of Clive's character as a failed father.

The progress in human relationships is also very obvious in the film: it begins with cool Will all alone in his trendy flat with only the TV for company and ends with a much warmer Will and his friends in the same flat enjoying a Christmas dinner together.

Humour, irony and sarcasm are also present in plenty in the film. Viewing the video or DVD will help to remind readers of the plot and the main themes. But watching the film – even twice or three times – is no substitute for reading the novel and enjoying its black humour.

Key Passages

The pages given in this list contain important passages on key themes. They are useful for revision purposes.

Will's views on family life: pp. 8–9
Marcus's problems at school: pp. 13–15
Will the Good Guy: pp. 20–21
"All men are bastards": pp. 35–36
Marcus's reaction to Fiona's suicide attempt: pp. 57–58
"Two wasn't enough": pp. 66–67
Will's empty life: pp. 71–73
Will's first thoughts on helping people: pp. 87–88
Marcus talks to Will about his school problems: pp. 98–99
Marcus talks to Will about his dad: pp. 104–105
Will enjoys buying Marcus a pair of trainers: pp. 110–112
Will loses his temper with Fiona: pp. 115–117
Marcus begins to think for himself: pp. 117–122
Will is still trying to shut life out: pp. 128–133
Will shows that he understands Marcus better than Fiona: pp. 130–133
Marcus's school situation improves: pp. 150–155
Will changes his mind about how to spend Christmas: p. 156
Scenes of embarrassment for Will: pp. 166–170
Marcus defends Will: pp. 169–170
Marcus's first real conversation with someone of his own age: pp. 181–183
Ellie's views on suicide as unfair to women: p. 182
Will decides to change his life: pp. 205–211
Will's reactions to Fiona's depression: pp. 212–215
Ellie's reaction to Kurt Cobain's attempted suicide: pp. 216–219
Will's crisis and the point of life: pp. 221–227
Fiona talks about her depression: pp. 244–245
Fiona makes a fool of herself at the police station: pp. 263–264
Marcus loses his temper with his parents: p. 264
Will's "mystical moment" of commitment: pp. 264–265
Marcus's "human pyramid" model: pp. 275–276
Losses and gains: p. 278

Question Time

1. *About a Boy* is a novel written by a man and dealing predominantly with male problems. Does the author give a fair or an unfair picture of female problems? List the problems facing Fiona, Suzie, Ellie and Rachel and discuss Hornby's portrayal of them.
2. "The situation in which Will Freeman is living at the beginning of the book is so untypical that the reader of the novel cannot see the relevance of the plot to our everyday lives." Discuss this critic's view with special reference to Will's problems.
3. What role do the social backgrounds of the main locations (London and Cambridge) play in creating the problems facing Marcus?
4. "It's no good being right when everybody else is wrong." What evidence can you find for this statement in the novel? Should we revise our ethical assessment of right and wrong?
5. "No man is an island" was the conclusion reached by the humanitarian priest and poet John Donne (1571–1631) in connection with the involvement of the individual in society as a whole. "I am an island," says Will in the film version of *About a Boy*. "I'm bloody Ibiza!" Which of them is right? Justify your view with reference to events in the story.
6. After Fiona's attempted suicide, Marcus comes to the conclusion that "two is not enough". Trace the development of Will's character through the book and show how he gradually comes to accept Marcus's conclusion.
7. *About a Boy* deals with serious, important human problems. At the same time, it is an extremely humorous narrative. Do you think that Hornby sometimes treats serious problems too flippantly? What are the main functions of humour in this book?
8. Fiona's lifestyle is governed by "alternative" principles. What principles, if any, guide the lives of the other main protagonists?
9. Would you say that Fiona is a good mother to Marcus? Give your reasons.
10. In what ways does Fiona manipulate her son? Does she really have a plan for him (pp. 118–119)?
11. In what way do you think changes in moral attitudes are responsible for many of the problematic situations described in the novel?
12. Ten years later: What developments do you think will have taken place by the time Will is 46 and Marcus is 22? Think about the other main characters, too.

Connections with other books or media items; suggestions for further studies

Nick Hornby's novel *How to Be Good* (2001) deals with interpersonal problems from the point of view of a female protagonist. Read as much of this novel as you need to make a comparison between the author's treatment of these problems.

The *Pleasure Principle* is the title of a 1991 British film, written, produced and directed by David Cohen and also set in London, about an amorous journalist who cannot decide which of the four women in his life is most important to him. Nick Hornby may well have seen this film before he wrote *About a Boy*. In philosophy and psychiatry, the pleasure principle is the natural human tendency to seek pleasure and avoid pain. This is Will's philosophy and is commonly known as hedonism. Trace and comment on examples of hedonism through the novel. If you have a chance to see a video or DVD of the film, compare it with the film of *About a Boy*.

Use the Internet to track down some of the singers and songs mentioned in the book. List them under the headings "Fiona's Music" and "Will's Music" and give them your own personal rating on a scale of 1 (very good) to 6 (don't like it much). You may be interested to check out Nick Hornby's personal musical taste in his book *31 Songs* (2003), which contains short essays on 31 popular songs and albums.

Answer Time

1. **Problems:**
   Fiona: single parent; depression; poor; can't find a suitable partner; firm alternative beliefs; "weird" son
   Suzie: single parent; poor; jobless (retraining as a nutritionist); having to look after her friend Fiona
   Ellie: daughter of a single parent; rebellious on principle
   Rachel: single parent; slightly neurotic son

   Hornby's treatment of female characters:
   On the whole, Hornby shows a deep understanding for the problems of his female characters, though he cannot resist poking fun at Fiona for her alternative beliefs, not only through Will (p. 131) but also through Marcus (p. 119). If we accept that Fiona is mainly responsible for Marcus's weirdness, we cannot say that Hornby, through his two main protagonists, treats her unfairly. Her naive remark to Will that "Marcus is doing fine" (p. 115) at school is accompanied by one of Will's rare outbursts of temper. Even when she has at last found out what is going on at school, her response to Marcus's statement: "Only Will knows what I need" is: "Don't be ridiculous. [...] We don't need that kind of person. We're doing all right our way." (pp. 117–118) Fiona simply is dithery and committed to absolute values which do not apply in Marcus's world. The best example of her "logic-free lectures" will be found on pp. 129–133.
   Suzie's bitterness is justified by the way her husband treated her (p. 35), and the description of male betrayal which follows is a fair introduction to the problems facing single mothers. Even Will's hopeful question: "So women do leave sometimes?" is demolished by Suzie's devastating reply: "Jeremy's wife was killed in a car crash." Suzie's revenge at Fiona's Christmas party is the "snubbing" scene which so fascinates Marcus (pp. 167–170). Her justifiable criticism that Will "pretends he has a child so he can join single parent groups and chat up single mothers" is seen as a relatively minor matter when Marcus, in defending Will, again highlights his own problems: "All he did was make up a kid for a couple of weeks. God. That's nothing. So what? Who cares? Kids at school do worse than that every day", and the whole "snubbing" episode ends on a humorous note with even Fiona and Suzie laughing when they are reminded of Dead Duck Day. Suzie also emphasizes the confusion facing a woman whose partner abandons her and his child (p. 52).

Ellie has an important role to play as Marcus's friend, protector and confidante. But unlike Marcus she enjoys her "shit life" and is justifiably unmasked as a person who protests against school and social injustice "just for the hell of it". Protest is, for her, a way of coping with life until she is old enough to make the kind of mistakes which the other adults in the novel have been making. It is ironical that the victim of her own main act of protest – the "exploitation" of Kurt Cobain's suicide – is a slightly older version of herself. At school she may seem to be a "guided missile", but in the outside world she is more like a bomb which might explode without warning and in any direction.
Ellie does, however, point out that there is an unfair (male chauvinist?) attitude towards women who commit or attempt to commit suicide (p. 182). The fact that Marcus thinks there is something wrong with her argument merely underlines the fact that many males fail to appreciate the pressures placed on women by their natural commitment to bringing up their children. Ellie also points out the unfairness of the mother's role in modern society: "At our school, there's about a million kids whose parents have split. And none of them are living with their dads" (p. 182). Thus Hornby shows sympathy for female problems here and elsewhere.
Rachel is the most stable single mother in the book. She is on top of her job as a children's book illustrator and can handle her slightly neurotic son. She is an optimist and has a great sense of humour. She understands Will's problems and helps him to solve them.
Will's thoughts on SPAT (p. 159) could summarize Hornby's picture of the problems of single parents: the SPAT meetings are not "full of happy but estranged couples" but "full of justified and righteous anger, and a very great deal of unhappiness".

2. Although Will's situation is almost unique, he has many character defects exhibited by men with 'normal', job-oriented lives: lack of commitment, fear of the pain of deep emotional entanglements etc. Hornby merely over-emphasizes Will's "island" (= self-oriented) nature by making him wealthy and relatively independent of normal social contacts (the "country full of things that Will knew nothing about and had no use for, like music therapists and housing officers and health-food shops with noticeboards [...] and difficult European novels and **feelings**", p. 105), a world of unemployment and poverty, though paradoxically Will is unemployed himself. This makes his gradual 'conversion' into a caring human being capable of deep emotions even more convincing. By taking an extreme example, Hornby not only highlights the problems within Will and society but also stresses that there is hope even for victims of worst-case scenarios.

3. **Cambridge**: small but world-famous university city (population 110,000 including 22,000 students); beautiful old city centre; pleasant suburbs; high level of culture and (international) multicultural activities; predominantly middle-class white population; plenty of "weird kids" and "weird mums" at Marcus's old school, where he has more friends (or at least fewer enemies).

   London: capital of the UK and largest city in Europe (population over 8 million); Marcus and his mother have moved to a lower-middle to working-class inner suburb; multicultural society; more peer-group pressure at school to conform to a trendy culture (clothes, haircuts, shoes, pop music) which Fiona rejects.

4. Marcus accepts his mother's values as right, and even other pupils at his school know that smoking and drug-taking is wrong, but the majority of people do not have Fiona's absolute convictions about right and wrong: most people think one thing and do another. In Marcus's house it is different. They decide what is bad and then they never touch it or do it again (see pp. 120–121). It is the conflict between what Fiona (and many other intelligent people) believe – or even know – to be right and the reality of the real world (which contains the vast majority of people) which is responsible for many of Marcus's problems. The fact of being right will not help you to survive in a society where most people do not share your opinion. Rightness and wrongness must not be confused with majority behaviour, particularly in a world where high-pressure advertising tries to influence what is right to listen to, eat, wear or watch on TV, and where pressure to conform to the peer group has never been stronger. Simply because the majority of young people wear Adidas trainers, have a certain type of haircut or listen to a certain type of music does not make them right in the moral or ethical sense. Fiona sticks to her ideas of right and wrong, which makes her intolerant of the shades of grey in between. One is reminded of the slogan "Two Legs – Bad, Four Legs – Good", from Orwell's novel *Animal Farm* and of the natural wish of most people (and *all* animals) to conform to majority behaviour or run the risk of becoming outsiders. Fiona thinks it is worth the risk, but she makes Marcus's school life miserable by forcing him to accept her arguments.

   Ethical assessment of right and wrong: Perhaps "right" and "wrong" are concepts which are too abstract for a society on which the emphasis is now on "(political) correctness". The term "correctness" (in the sense of replacing negatively-loaded words like "fat", "illiterate" and "lazy person" with positive-sounding terms such as "horizontally-challenged", "lexically-challenged" and "under-achiever") is rapidly replacing "right" (in the sense of 'human rights'). Such absolute values as right and wrong seem to have less relevance in a multicultural society where all kinds of opinions have to be equally respected. There is no need to assess the ethical validity of right and wrong, simply their usefulness as values in today's society. It is the values of today's society, perhaps, (coolness, trendiness, fashion, popular taste in music etc.) not our basic ethical values (right and wrong) that require re-assessment.

5. The whole progression of the novel leaves the reader in no doubt as to which of these opposing opinions is morally and ethically right. Will develops from a selfish lone wolf who despises the family unit to the caring, emotionally involved human being who finally realizes that life is "like air" and that there is "no way of shutting it out" (p. 256). Marcus undergoes a similar transformation: from the geeky outsider with no friends at school to the wise 'philosopher' with his theories on the future of couples and the "human pyramid". From the moment Will and Marcus meet, Will is involved in other people's problems (Fiona's attempted suicide, Marcus's problems at school, even Rachel's search for a suitable partner) and Marcus begins to see possible solutions to his dilemmas (Will gets him out of trouble with the park-keeper on Dead Duck Day, drives him to the hospital after Fiona's suicide attempt, puts up with his after-school visits when Marcus is afraid to go home in case his mother has "done it" again, explains about Kirk O'Bane – indirectly helping Marcus to get to know Ellie better –, plays a different kind of music to him, buys him the right trainers and so on). Will even begins to enjoy making these unselfish gestures, describing his feelings after the purchase of the trainers as a "natural high" (p. 112).
   The mutual benefits of such involvement in other people's problems are obvious to the reader of the novel. They far outweigh the selfish benefits of the "island existence".

6. At the beginning of the novel, Will's character is so shallow that it hardly deserves the name. Will's original philosophy is: one (= me) is plenty. Two (= me plus partner) is risky and can lead to pain. Three (couple + child/children) is "clutter" (p. 7) which leads to disaster. It is obvious that he considers himself (as he says in the film version) "the star of The Will Show", with the rest of the human race in walk-on roles. He has few real friends (two of whom he ditches in Chapter 2) and his relationships with women (after a longish affair with Jessica) are superficial and of short duration. His encounter with Marcus awakens a feeling of compassion and a desire to help a boy who is so alone

in the world. He decides perhaps that "good works" (p. 88), helping people, might be a new way forward for him: helping Fiona and her son. But such good works are still very ego-centred ("he'd helped Angie by sleeping with her")! He gradually admits that he "had spent his whole life avoiding real stuff" (p. 104). Marcus, on the other hand, has to face real stuff at school every day. "Sometimes Marcus sounded as though he were a hundred years old, and it broke Will's heart" (p. 109). So slowly, against his own belief that "no problem was his problem" (p. 106), Will's character changes for the better, and Fiona soon makes it clear to him that he has become involved in Marcus's life: "He's living this whole life I can't control, which means you have to" (p. 133). At this stage in the novel, Will can still reject this view: "She was wrong, he was almost positive. You could shut life out. If you didn't answer the door to it, how was it going to get in?"

When Will sees Marcus playing truant after the Mrs Morrison episode, he has an amusing fight with his conscience (see p. 143). But the implication is clear: half way through the book Will has developed far enough to listen to the voice of his conscience.

Will's realization that Marcus does not need a father figure as a model but "help to be a kid" (p. 147) gives his life much more meaning. When Christmas arrives, Will's character has developed enough for him to realize that spending Christmas on his own "didn't seem very festive, somehow and [...] spending three days bombed out of your head on your own said things about you that you might not want saying" (p. 156). When Will falls in love with Rachel, he decides to end his isolation. He wants Rachel to be more than just another girlfriend. He wants her "to be his wife, his lover, the centre of his whole world" (p. 189). Will realizes how empty his life is: the only things that have made him interesting so far have been his two 'invented' children: Ned and Marcus. So far Will has been helping Marcus, but now the roles are reversed: Marcus is able to help Will by pretending to be his son, and in conversation with Rachel Will realizes, almost with shock, that Marcus has real feelings towards him. This marks a further development in Will's character: the capacity to receive, as well as give, affection: "Rachel's observation that there were real feelings involved kind of changed things" (p. 224). This conversation with Rachel also brings Will face to face with his loneliness and the pointlessness of his life. Showing great understanding, Rachel explains "the point" (p. 226), and Will now realizes that there must surely be more of a point to life than just waiting for a new Nirvana album to come out or watching the next episode of *NYPD Blue*.

Will becomes more involved in the lives and problems of more people. He is able to tackle Fiona's new attack of depression by simply being a good listener. They go to the Pizza Express on Upper Street where he had used to meet Jessica, and Will looks back at the time "before SPAT and Marcus and Suzie and Fiona and Rachel and everything. He'd been an idiot then, but at least he'd been an idiot with an idea, some kind of belief system; now he was hundreds of years older [...]. He'd had his whole life set up so that nobody's problem was his problem, and now everybody's problem was his problem" (pp. 242–243). But he seems to be accepting this fact now.

When Marcus and Ellie get into trouble with the police on their way to Cambridge, Will finally realizes that he can no longer shut life out. He is no longer viewing life through a window, life as a soap opera, life as expressed only in soulful jazz or angry rap songs. In the car on the way to Royston there is an atmosphere of "despair, shared concern, suppressed hysteria, and straightforward team spirit – and Will could feel that he was inside it" (p. 258). He is no longer an "outsider" living on an island of his own. At the police station he is given "a glimpse of what it was like to be human. It wasn't too bad, really; he wouldn't even mind being human on a full-time basis" (pp. 265–265). At the end of Chapter 34, Will finally rejects his old self: "This thing about looking for someone less different ... It only really worked, he realized, if you were convinced that being you wasn't so bad in the first place." (p. 266) His relationship with Rachel depends on changing all his previous ideas about himself. Only then can he become "less different" enough to deserve Rachel. Despite the fear of disappointment, he wants Rachel so much that he knows he cannot go back: "that part of his life was over" (p. 273).

So at the end of the novel we see Will taking Ali and Marcus out on Saturdays – even for lunch at hamburger restaurants where one wonders whether Marcus the Vegetarian can resist a cheeseburger or a greasy double whopper. The old tone of Will's shallow, 'flip' and 'pseud' conversation with its meaningless "throwaway one-liners" (p. 242) is no match even for Marcus now. When Marcus expresses his views on couples and the family, all Will can think of saying is: "Oh, well thank you ... Einstein." Marcus's reply: "What's he got to do with it?" (p. 276) demolishes Will's objections to his theories. The final conclusion is that "Will had lost his shell and his cool and his distance, and he felt scared and vulnerable, but he got to be with Rachel" (p. 278), so he has finally rejected his "one person is enough" philosophy.

7. The main functions of humour – not just in this book – are to produce a spontaneous emotional feeling (a smile or laughter) in the viewer, listener or reader. The appeal to the emotions is much stronger in

most people than the appeal to intelligence via logical argument. It is more fun to read a 'funny' book than to read a school textbook, for example. And we remember comical explanations more easily than factual explanations. Fiona, for example, justifies her vegetarianism not by putting forward the standard arguments but by telling Marcus: "I didn't decide on the spur of the moment because we'd run out of sausages." (p. 119) We smile, and remember the situation more easily. Humour works immediately and directly. The way in which Will divides his day into half-hour units (though it is a sad comment on the quality of his empty life) is made memorable by the inclusion of the comic activity of "doing a quick crossword on the toilet". This is perhaps the only 'activity' which the reader remembers from the list, and its humorous nature emphasizes the emptiness of Will's well-structured life better than any moralizing comment about time-wasting.
Humour also makes serious and potentially tragic situations more bearable. There is no humour in Fiona's suicide attempt, but when Will says "If I were about to stick my head in the gas oven, and then you told me Marcus adored me, I wouldn't necessarily take it out again" (p. 225), Rachel bursts out laughing, saying that if she were there in such a situation, she would have to conclude that their evening together had not been a success.
Unintentionally humorous remarks help to relieve tense situations: when Lindsey asks, politely, what Will does for a living, Marcus says: "He doesn't do anything ... his father wrote 'Santa's Super Sleigh' and he earns a million pounds a minute" (comic exaggeration). Suzie immediately emphasizes the negative side of Will's shallow life by saying that he "pretends he has a child so he can join single parent groups and chat up single mothers". Marcus's naive comment is: "Yeah, but he doesn't get paid for that" (p. 169). The reader smiles, but the comic tone of the naive comment emphasizes Will's position in society. He may think of himself as an island; other people would tend to see him (in social and human terms) as "a waste of space".
Marcus's lack of achievement in his new environment is heavily underlined by the killing of a duck during the SPAT picnic. This is the first time he has succeeded in doing *anything* he has seriously tried to do: not to *kill* the duck, of course, only to *hit* it with a piece of bread. Despite the irony, this not very humorous action is not shown in a tragic context. His announcement of his 'success' comes immediately after Will's indirect request to Suzie that she should become his girlfriend. The comic element increases when, despite Marcus's exaggerated fears that "he'd be imprisoned for a crime he never committed", they go to examine the dead duck and Will remarks to the park-keeper: "One of your ducks has died", making it "sound as if it were the saddest thing

he'd ever seen" (p.55). When, instead of calling the police, the park-keeper sadly remarks: "I'll have to wade in and get it", there is a fine sense of anti-climax. The relief expressed in the lines: "They were in the clear. Marcus wasn't going to jail for a crime he probably – OK, possibly – didn't commit" is comic because of the exaggeration of the seriousness of the original situation. But this humorous episode is followed immediately by the discovery that Fiona has tried to kill herself, so humour here is skilfully used to stress potential tragedy by a sudden shift of mood (from comedy to tragedy in less than one page).

We smile at Marcus's naive comments throughout the book. Although we are told he does not appreciate or understand sarcasm, he uses it to torpedo Will's well-intentioned attempts to "strike up a sparky, mutually curious relationship" by asking if Will is "getting these questions out of a book" (p. 49). Suzie laughs and Will – who hates embarrassment of any kind – blushes. When asked who his favourite singer is, Marcus replies "Joni Mitchell" and goes on to pretend that everybody at school likes her, thus adding to Will's confusion. So even Marcus has a sense of humour, though there is little evidence of it most of the time.

There is much slapstick comedy in the scene at Royston police station: Fiona overdramatically defends Marcus as if he had committed a serious crime; Clive gives a display of righteous indignation about Ellie's behaviour that contrasts comically with his casual University of Life T-shirt and plaster cast. Ellie puts up a fight for human rights before being confronted by the victim of her attack on the shop window: a five-years-older double wearing the same Kurt Cobain T-shirt! Marcus tells his mother to shut up and says he can't believe how crap his parents are. The police officers are smiling and obviously enjoying themselves. It is indeed a pity that this scene was not included in the film.

The person with the best sense of humour in the book is undoubtedly Rachel. In a situation where Fiona would have expressed anger – the embarrassing scene where Will is trying to explain his complicated "relationship" with Marcus – she reacts to Will's half-truths in a different, but equally firm way: "If I want to be amused and tolerant, that's my business. I'm not yet at a stage where you can make jokes, too. […] But where does Marcus come in? I mean, you obviously hadn't hired him for the afternoon. There's some kind of relationship there" (p. 209). Her witty insertion of the idea of "hiring" a child for the afternoon makes it easier for Will to show her that he is involved in Marcus's life and cares about him.

8. **Guiding principles:**
Will: self-indulgence; avoidance of embarrassment and disappointment; aloofness (at the start of the novel)
Marcus: self-preservation (by keeping a low profile at school and trying to "find more people")
Ellie: revolt against authority
Rachel: optimism, tolerance

9. **Positive sides of Fiona as a mother:**
   - She tries to protect her son against negative influences (= Will).
   - She gives him healthy food to eat and warm (unfashionable) clothes to wear.
   - Like most parents, she wants the best for her son. But she has her own inflexible ideas about what is best.
   - She worries about her adequacy as a single parent (p. 130).
   - She furiously defends him at the police station.

   Negative sides of Fiona as a mother:
   - She is authoritarian and imposes her views on her son.
   - She has a black-and-white view of right and wrong.
   - She suffers from depressions and becomes just "the woman under the coat" at times.
   - She fails to understand Marcus's school problems and his other needs.

10. Fiona manipulates Marcus by using logical arguments which he has to accept: "too expensive, too late, too young, bad for your teeth, the other [TV] channel, homework, fruit" (p. 2). Although she tells him she wants him to think for himself, she really wants him to think like her. Marcus is naive in believing she has a plan for him simply because she is his mother. On p. 121, when he asks her about her plan, she becomes confused: "Did I say that? [...] Well, of course I want you to think for yourself. All parents want that." She only tries to bring Will into their lives because she sees that Marcus is "living this whole life which I can't control" (p. 133), so the main idea behind her plan seems to be to control her son, either alone or with another person's help. At the end of the book, she feels she is losing her son, although she has to admit that the new version of Marcus is easier for her to handle. She gives up trying to manipulate him and becomes a healthier, saner mother as a result.

11. **Moral attitudes in Britain have relaxed over the past half century and, in combination with the rise of women's liberation movements, this has led to the following changes, best viewed in the form of a table:**

	1950s – 1970s	Today
Smoking:	forbidden at school; "bad for your health"; smoking stops you from growing	not for under-16s; tobacco not to be sold to under-12s; SMOKING KILLS on every packet
School:	strict rules, uniforms, less peer-group pressure because of uniforms	less-strict rules, dress code (clothing guidelines), no physical contact between teachers and pupils, peer-group pressure
Drug abuse:	practically unknown	marihuana (pot) may be smoked, but not in public
Alcohol:	nobody under 18 allowed to drink in a pub; alcohol only sold at special outlets ("off licences") to adult customers	drinking age is still 18 in pubs; all types of alcohol readily available in shops and supermarkets
Sex before marriage:	absolutely taboo (too dangerous! Condoms only usually sold "under the counter" at *men's* barber shops or by mail order to married couples); fear of infection and associated social stigma	not for the under-15s (officially 16); practise "safe sex" (condoms available at any supermarket); medical help easily available
Sex education:	"reproduction in mammals" during school biology lessons (rabbit, etc.); perhaps a few informal talks from an embarrassed parent	official school subject; widespread coverage of "explicit" sex in all the media; "topless" women in every tabloid newspaper on "Page 3"
Partnership:	marriage: husband goes to work, wife gives up job, life-long partnership, divorce was unusual and difficult/expensive to obtain; husband was expected to "support" his wife and family financially (husband = breadwinner; wife = home-maker)	marriage not essential; partners without children usually both work, length of partnership very flexible, a divorce is now much simpler and cheaper to get; far more social services and welfare payments for single parents; no fixed roles (John is on "paternity leave", Christine goes to work)

	1950s–1970s	Today
Having children:	get married first; make sure you can afford them! Give them a good home; unmarried mothers often went into special homes until their children were born – and adopted by "respectable" couples	no discrimination of single parents (usually mothers), so no special protection for single mothers
Parental authority:	*Mum:* "Just wait till I tell your dad what you did!"	*Kid:* "Touch me, and I'll call the Child Welfare people or the police!"
Equality of the genders:	women had fewer rights and had no job equality, their pay in the jobs open to them was often lower because they were not breadwinners	women are officially "equal" but are still often paid less than men for the same work

Results: men have become more mobile; women take on the double role of parenting (a new concept) and going to work – they cannot complain as much as in the old days because they are equal and emancipated and looked after by the social services; emancipation has brought not only benefits to women but also many disadvantages.
Increasing concern about children's rights has reduced the authority of parents, teachers and the police.
A more permissive attitude towards sex, drugs and alcohol consumption together with more help for people with resultant problems has weakened or even removed the traditional foundations of the family unit. As Marcus realizes, two is not enough if one of them is a child and the other is unstable.

12. **Best-case scenario:**
Will is happily married to Rachel and they have two lovely children of their own. Rachel still illustrates children's books and Will has a fulfilling part-time job at the offices of a Third-World charity organization, helping people. Marcus and Ali are studying at university. Fiona has found a new partner (a former hippy, like herself). Suzie is a successful dietician. Clive has a senior position with Cambridge Social Services and Lindsey is happy at home with her two young children. Ellie has teamed up with Ruth at the Royston music shop and sings with a local pop group called Worzel Gummidge (which is, in fact, the name of a children's television character, a scarecrow, from the 1980s; see annotation on p. 281). "Santa's Super Sleigh" has disappeared from the charts.

Worst-case scenario:
Will and Rachel have split up after several happy years. Will's drug habit has got worse: he now takes hard drugs and is desperately unhappy. Rachel is still an optimist and works hard, but it is difficult bringing up her small daughter without a father. Marcus is working as a chartered accountant (see p. 49) and is bored stiff with his job. Ali is out of work and in psychiatric care. Fiona still suffers from depression and is very lonely now that Marcus has left home. She still sings Joni Mitchell songs with her eyes closed. Suzie is still out of work. She is now "retraining" as a chiropodist (= Fußpflegerin). Clive is still a badly paid social worker. He and Lindsey have four lovely children. Clive is overworked and gets little sleep at night. He is nearly fifty and gets up at 2 a.m. to feed their new baby. Ellie has abandoned rebellion. She has her hands full with her young family. Her partner is a roadie with a successful pop group (see p. 150), owns a Harley-Davidson motorbike which he never has time to ride and is only at home two days a week.

Lektürehilfen – Literatur verstehen

Lektürehilfen sind der Schlüssel zum besseren Verständnis von Literatur:

- Die wichtigen Themen kennen dank thematischer Kapitel.
- Die richtigen Antworten wissen durch die Vorbereitung mit typischen Abiturfragen.
- Inhaltsangabe der Lektüre als mp3-Download unter: www.klett.de/lernhilfen

Paul Auster
Moon Palace
ISBN 978-3-12-923046-6 | 9,95 €

T. C. Boyle
Tortilla Curtain
ISBN 978-3-12-923001-5 | 9,95 €

Ray Bradbury
Fahrenheit 451
ISBN 978-3-12-923050-3 | 9,95 €

Caught between Cultures
ISBN 978-3-12-923016-9 | 9,95 €

Don DeLillo
Falling Man
ISBN 978-3-12-923053-4 | 9,95 €

Nick Hornby
About a Boy
ISBN 978-3-12-923003-9 | 9,95 €

Arthur Miller
Death of a Salesman
ISBN 978-3-12-923048-0 | 9,95 €

Willy Russell
Educating Rita
ISBN 978-3-12-923028-2 | 9,95 €

William Shakespeare
Romeo and Juliet
ISBN 978-3-12-923039-8 | 9,95 €

Macbeth
ISBN 978-3-12-923038-1 | 9,95 €

Tennessee Williams
A Streetcar Named Desire
ISBN 978-3-12-923045-9 | 9,95 €

Im Buchhandel erhältlich. **Weitere Informationen unter www.klett.de/lernhilfen**